EQUALITY, TOLERANCE, AND LOYALTY

Also by Andrew R. Cecil:

The Third Way: Enlightened Capitalism and the
Search for a New Social Order

The Foundations of a Free Society

Three Sources of National Strength

Equality
Tolerance
and
Loyalty

Virtues Serving the
Common Purpose of Democracy

By

Andrew R. Cecil

Supplement to
The Andrew R. Cecil Lectures on Moral Values
in a Free Society

The University of Texas at Dallas
1990

Library of Congress Catalog Card Number 89-051995
International Standard Book Number 0-292-72074-2

Distributed by The University of Texas Press,
Box 7819, Austin, Texas 78712

To my daughter, Christine

FOREWORD

This book is the third Supplement to its annual proceedings of the Andrew R. Cecil Lectures on Moral Values in a Free Society that The University of Texas at Dallas has published. Like the previous two supplement volumes, it consists of essays by Dr. Andrew R. Cecil for whom the Lectures are named. It represents the capstone of his thoughts which have graced the series since its inception.

In 1979, when Dr. Cecil retired as Chancellor of The Southwestern Legal Foundation, the University invited him to serve as its Distinguished Scholar in Residence and established the Andrew R. Cecil Lectures on Moral Values in a Free Society. This program was founded on the premise that a university has a responsibility that goes beyond those other essential missions of providing excellent professional preparation for its students and of establishing an environment where vital research may be carried out. An institution of higher learning must also provide a forum for the discussion and debate of important issues confronting its society. Examining questions of values and of moral obligations is an essential part of a university's business. To these ends the Lectures on Moral Values in a Free Society were instituted, and they have become an important tradition in the life of our campus.

The Lectures were named for Dr. Cecil because he has consistently addressed throughout his career these fundamental moral issues. In his work as a writer, educator, and administrator in the fields of law and economics he has always stressed his abiding belief in the dignity and worth of the human individual.

Since the inception of the Lectures, Dr. Cecil has taken an active interest in the series and has been a primary force in assuring its success. At the request of the University he delivered the inaugural series of the Lectures in November 1979. The proceedings of that series were made permanently available as Volume I of the Andrew R. Cecil Lectures on Moral Values in a Free Society, *The Third Way: Enlightened Capitalism and the Search for a New Social Order.* That book offers Dr. Cecil's analysis of the moral under-pinnings of our economic and social order. The seven lectures that comprise it address such varied topics as economics and Christian ethics, dogmas and moral values, and the striving for self-determination and basic human rights throughout the world.

Dr. Cecil has lectured in each of the subsequent series—which by the autumn of 1989 numbered eleven in all. In 1983, the University published a book by Dr. Cecil that provided an important extension of the ideas in *The Third Way* as the first supplement to the series of the proceedings. That book was entitled *The Foundations of a Free Society* because it explored the bedrock on which our liberties are founded: morality and religion, justice and natural rights, knowledge and education. Just as *The Third Way* stressed that there must be a path to social organizations far removed from totalitarian control as well as from heedless individualism, *The Foundations of a Free Society* stressed that restraint and responsibility are essential prerequisites to true liberty.

In 1986, the University published a second supplementary book authored by Dr. Cecil, *Three Sources of National Strength*. That book pursued the question of what truly makes a country strong, and stressed that military might alone cannot ensure a country's greatness. Dr. Cecil argues that the actual source of our nation's unique qualities are such intangible qualities as the spirit of freedom, patriotism, and economic stability.

Now the University presents a new supplementary volume—which Dr. Cecil envisions will be the final one in this series—that examines the question of how a nation achieves a common purpose and stresses the virtues that undergird and serve the common purpose of democracy. Together with the three previous volumes in the series by Dr. Cecil it is part of a single argument. Dr. Cecil contends that our country does not accomplish the goal of a common purpose by means of coercion or indoctrination as totalitarian countries do. As Dr. Cecil points out, we hold up the ideals of equality, tolerance, and loyalty. This decade in which the Andrew R. Cecil Lectures have sought to help reignite faith in these ideals in our own society has also seen a great rekindling of such a faith around the world. As Dr. Cecil and the other lecturers who have appeared in the series have repeatedly pointed out, these are ideals with a universal significance and appeal.

The University can look with great pride on the record that The Andrew R. Cecil Lectures on Moral Values in a Free Society has established over the last eleven years. Nearly fifty outstanding scholars, statesmen, and business leaders of national and international reputation have presented lectures on a high plane of distinction. These lectures have offered wisdom and insight for all those who have heard them or read them in their printed form. The published proceedings offer a distinctive repository of the ruminations of persons of substantial achievement on a subject that is too often taken for granted: the moral foundations of our culture. These books have met with an enthusiastic response and are widely used by students and faculty in universities, colleges, and secondary schools throughout the nation.

The University owes a debt of gratitude to the donors who have made this important program possible. Their generosity and farsightedness have enabled the University to establish and maintain a valued tradition and to fulfill its goal of shedding light on our moral heritage.

I also wish to take this opportunity to express the University's appreciation to Dr. Cecil himself. As this book goes to press, the University is establishing an Endowed Chair in Applied Ethics to bear Dr. Cecil's name. Such a chair will be a means of ensuring that Dr. Cecil's work in examining important ethical questions is extended beyond his own active involvement, and its establishment is designed to honor Dr. Cecil for his fifty years of educational service.

The publication of this book, *Equality, Tolerance, and Loyalty: Virtues Serving the Common Purpose of Democracy*, also fittingly honors its author on the occasion of the fiftieth anniversary of the beginning of his academic career. Its contents conveniently display the qualities of thought and feeling for which we honor him.

ROBERT H. RUTFORD, President
The University of Texas at Dallas
November, 1989

CONTENTS

CONTENTS (continued)

INTRODUCTION

Following the precedent set by titling my previous book *Three Sources of National Strength*, I thought of calling this volume *Three Sources of Democracy's Strength*, but—wisely or not—I gave up this idea for several reasons. First is the fact that the principles of equality, tolerance, and loyalty discussed in this book are only three strands in the majestic robe of democracy in which other moral values are woven together. The unraveling of only three moral issues—even if they are among the main strands of democracy— might wrongfully imply that they alone mark democracy in its essence.

The second reason concerns the numerous senses in which the term "democracy" is used: as the participation of all citizens, rich and poor, in electing their representative government; as the guarantee of each citizen's equality before the law; as social and economic opportunity with an egalitarian tendency to create a free society of equals; or as the consent of the governed who see in the protection of both freedom and the dignity of man the chief aim of government.

Third, pure democracy has never existed, and there will never be a perfect democracy that will correspond to a universally accepted ideological model. There has never been a society where all the people exercised the same authority to govern. In Athens— often considered the cradle of democracy—not all the people had the capability of acting directly or through representatives to control the state's institutions. The rights of citizenship were exercised by fewer than half of the adult males in the population, with women, slaves, aliens, and outlaws being excluded.

Plato rejected the concept of democracy. He was afraid that the poor would always control a democracy. In *The Republic* he advocated a system that combined what he saw as the best qualities of monarchy and aristocracy. Aristotle also had reservations about the idea of democracy, accepting it as the lesser of evils. He preferred to leave the practical matters of government in the hands of the wealthy, who could offer their time and talents to public affairs; but in order to preserve stability through moderation, Aristotle recommended a constitutional government or polity that combines the merits of democracy and oligarchy.

In Rome, though the state was formally a *res publica*—a "public affair"—the authority that the term implied was vested in the people was, as a rule, ignored by the emperor. The division of the Roman people into patricians and plebeians became a source of serious conflicts. Only through compromises and political concessions did the plebeians make constitutional gains that ended the patricio-plebeian struggle.

Until the nineteenth century, when the idea of democracy began to gain popularity, traces of sharp division between the rich and the poor, the oppressors and the oppressed, the privileged nobility and the underprivileged common man could be seen throughout the Western world. The "Great American Experiment," which Thomas Jefferson compared to a "ball of liberty" that would "roll around the globe," addressed the right to liberty, leaving open the question of governance.

It was the Bill of Rights that moved the emerging states in our own nation toward democracy. Still, most of those who wrote "We the People" were men of substance who felt that only the "well born" could be entrusted with the responsibility of government. John Adams, in his suggestion of a bicameral legislature, sought a balance between "aristocracy" and the "common man." It was Jefferson who contrasted "an artificial aristocracy founded on wealth and birth without either virtue or talents" with "natural aristocracy" based on "virtue and talents," which are "the most precious gift of nature."

This distinction between "natural" and "artificial" aristocracy gave the new nation a singular position among the nations existing at the time of its birth. Wealth, or what Jefferson called "the old aristocratic interest" of the "well born"—in spite of the expectations of some of the Founding Fathers who feared democracy—was not the qualification for discharging the responsibilities of government.

This distinction also protected the new democracy against the danger of egalitarianism. Although no citizen could be excluded by birth or wealth from voting for persons of his choice to fill government office, the best form of government, according to Jefferson, is the government "that provides most effectively for a pure selection of these natural 'aristoi' into the offices of the government."

In modern times we have witnessed the deplorable counterfeit of democracy by communist tyrants insisting that their system of government is of a democratic nature. "Democratic Republics" or "Peoples' Democracies" have spread throughout the communist world, which uses the words "freedom" and "democracy" as tools of oppression and to impose tyranny. Dictators, under the disguise of offering democracy and liberation, have invaded other countries and deprived the conquered nations of individual liberty, claiming that dictatorship is a necessary transition to democracy. This "transition" in Soviet Russia is still taking place, although more than 70 years have passed since the Bolshevik Revolution. Communism, like any other form of absolutism, cannot coexist with the individual liberty that is indispensable for democracy to succeed. Recent events in the People's Republic of China give testimony that tyranny cannot tolerate any attempt to fulfill the natural human desire for freedom.

In China, when the government faced the choice between accommodating the very limited demands for freedom and maintaining the totalitarian nature of the regime, it chose tyranny and the massacre of thousands. The Chinese government rejected the idea of slow evolution toward more democracy and less corruption that had been adopted by Soviet Russia and Poland and launched a brutal assault against its own people, reminding us of the Stalinist terror during which family members denounced their parents, sons, and brothers. The exact number killed and arrested may never be known.

In the revolt against communism in Poland, in the first democratic election since 1947, the opposition party Solidarity whipped the communist party. This victory reflected the voice of a people permitted to participate in a democratic experience unique in the communist world.

Confusing independence with democracy may create another counterfeit of democracy. As much as we detest colonization, the fact remains that some of the colonies that gained political independence produced, not democracy, but tyranny followed by chaos and the savage slaughter of members of the tribes unfriendly to the dictator's tribe. The principles that launched the struggle for independence consumed each other.

Democracy is not a dogma, and so the moral issues discussed in this volume are not dogmas limited to a certain place and time. Throughout recent history, we have witnessed the ascent and eventual fall of many dogmas that tried to offer a vision of a perfect society. In order not to suffer the fate of these passing dogmas, each generation has to breathe new life into democracy and its main strands. Otherwise, we may find that the moral issues essential for democracy may conflict with each other.

Freedom may conflict with equality. Down the road of total freedom lies a mistaken idea of freedom that leads to fragmentation and self-interest. When freedom is not understood as an opportunity for people to make moral, responsible decisions, it may mean license for the powerful to oppress and exploit the weak who yearn for equality. Unbridled freedom may be in conflict with the principle of equality explained by Thomas Paine when he said, "The principle of equality of rights is quite simple. Every man can understand it, and it is by understanding his rights that he learns his duties; for where the rights of men are equal, every man must finally see the necessity of protecting the rights of others as the most effective security of his own."

If the powerful stress liberty, the underprivileged demand equality. If Patrick Henry exclaimed his readiness to die for liberty, the poor and weak may be found ready to express their willingness to die for equality, more equal distribution of economic benefits, social status, and political power. The stride toward equality does not, however, require an egalitarianism that rejects the moral standards that safeguard society against cultural degeneration and sterility. Equality before the law protects the dignity of the individual, regardless of both his or her occupation and the material resources available. This does not mean that in a society of equals before the law all individuals are born with equal faculties and talents. As John Adams, recognizing the truth that all people are born to equal rights, also warned, to teach that all people are born with equal powers and faculties is a "gross fraud." A free society is destined to have some acceptable levels of inequality associated with individual creativity, efficiency, knowledge, and abilities.

Tolerance, the fundamental principle of democracy, is, like freedom, not absolute. The rules of constitutional procedure demand that we are tolerant of those with whom we disagree. No economic order or legal system is faultless. No form of government is perfect and beyond improvement. Democracy is not a manifestation of political perfection; it is subject to evolutionary adjustment, to social changes, and to technological and other new advances that occur.

The dynamic principle of democracy may tend to create different versions of a democratic society. We may, therefore, expect that, because of the uncertainty of human understanding, we will find differences of opinion. Conflict of ideas, however, is not a sign of weakness in democracy. The freedom to criticize and to disagree is a sign of democracy's strength. Persistent search for truth means liberty of the mind. Through experience we can recognize partial truth, but no one can claim the possession of the absolute truth. Democracy distrusts all absolute claims but gives every individual the right to aspire to the truth as long as he or she does not deny this right to anyone else.

The highest value of democracy is the effort to find the truth through competition and the testing of ideas, but tolerance cannot be extended to those who are determined to destroy that value. There are limits to tolerance. The best test of truth, as Justice Oliver Wendell Holmes pointed out, "is the power of the thought to get itself accepted in the competition of the market"; but where such thoughts tend to unleash division in a society— a division that may lead to riots and destruction—tolerance should be exercised only within limits of the preservation of public order and of legitimate constitutional procedures. There is a fine line between the creative power of tolerance and the license to destroy. As paradoxical as it may sound, intolerance of intolerance defends tolerance, while tolerance of intolerance defeats the principle of tolerance and with it one of the essential prerequisites of democracy.

Equality—which, as we mentioned, may conflict with liberty—is far from being absolute. In times of economic catastrophe (such as during the Great Depression), some had the misconception that socialization of all major means of production and increased governmental control would remove disparities of wealth, assure more equality, and contribute to a better society. Today, we have enough knowledge of what happens under a totalitarian regime to alert us to the danger of this misconception of equality, which produced, not prosperity, but misery, poverty, and dictatorship. In sacrificing the dignity and sacredness of the individual human personality, totalitarian regimes substitute slavery for equality. To dictatorship unrestricted by law—which uses force, coercion, and violence to liquidate all elements that might be discordant—equality means institutionalized torture and prison as the penalty for dissenting with the regime; it means that all persons are to be regarded as economic expendables and commodities.

By leveling all to one standard, we may obtain only an equal share of poverty; we may not lift the underprivileged to have their share of prosperity. We do not produce prosperity by reducing the superior performer to the level of the less talented. This, of course, does not mean that we should not be concerned about the welfare of our fellowmen. In the United States, among the dramatic strides in the direction of such concern for equality have been universal suffrage, which gave equal voting privileges to all, regardless of sex, race, or color; progressive taxation; public education; Social Security, Medicare, and social welfare programs; and the recent civil rights legislation.

The growth of expectation of equality is, however, greater than the growth of our resources. There is a dismaying gap between what we expect from our government and the resources available to the government to meet our expectations. We enjoy more material goods than the generations preceding us, we live longer in a healthier environment, we are better paid for our work since we are better educated and more literate, yet we continue to express our discontent. We complain about the smog, the polluted streams and rivers, the slums in the cities, inadequate housing, and overcrowded hospitals. When the lakes are clean enough to swim in, we complain that the water is not clean enough to drink. We drive our cars that cause air pollution but refuse to use mass transportation that should reduce such pollution.

Alexis de Tocqueville foresaw this discontent when he wrote:

> "The evil which was suffered patiently as inevitable seems unendurable as soon as the idea of escaping from it crosses men's minds. All the abuses then removed call attention to those that remain, and they now appear more galling. The evil, it is true, has become less, but sensibility to it has become more acute."

The expected governmental responsibility and services make social man a political man. The public spirit of the "political man" and his concern about the welfare of his country make him a partaker in the government. Against the advantage of wealth, the right to vote gives the "little" man the advantage of carrying out his powers of choice, of carrying out his political wishes. Political equality, through the right to vote, has expanded the citizen's opportunity to improve his economic and political condition.

Participation in issues concerning government makes democracy live and function. The substance of democracy is, however, lacking when the voters cast their votes in ignorance. It is the role of education to adequately prepare the citizen to function in a democratic society by participating intelligently and rationally in creating a government dedicated to serve. When the voter, rich or poor, is swayed by emotion, prejudice, or unquestioned preconceptions, the right to vote is an empty if not harmful privilege that curtails and perhaps suspends the principles of liberty, equality, and tolerance in a free society.

The substance of democracy is also lacking when citizens feel no loyalty to this form of government. Loyalty is one of the working principles of democracy, since it compresses the high purposes, the deep feelings, and the aspirations that unite citizens under one banner of faith in human dignity. It does not exist in a vacuum; it means commitment to something. This "something" in a democracy is a just, common purpose that binds citizens together and makes moral demands on their actions and attitudes.

Like tolerance and equality, loyalty to a just and common purpose is not absolute. It is endangered by the coexistence of other, competing loyalties to racial, religious, and economic groups, to family, and to friends. It also faces conflicts that cause the so-called loyalty controversies, to mention only the problems of loyalty to the "City of God" or to the "City of Man," to the state or to a family, to the country or to a friend.

A "just purpose" should be the central motive of loyalty. Without such a purpose, loyalty may be exploited for unworthy aims. Allegiance to Hitler, Stalin, or other tyrants hardly can be praised as a virtue. Those who surrender their conscience to totalitarian governments and serve as their tools of oppression act as accomplices to crime. Only a just purpose justifies the loyalty that is definable as a high moral standard calling for actions of benefit to our fellowman.

Loyalty, tolerance, and equality are integral parts of our democratic institutions. Democracy works on behalf of human dignity and human worth. It is the only form of government that allows and cultivates human dignity. The three "strands" in the majestic robe of democracy discussed in this book are the timeless tenets of human conduct indispensable for a nation to remain free. They unravel the individual's sense of self-worth, his self-discipline, his freedom to choose among the countless causes that exist in a free society, and his recognition of the duty to preserve the social order that makes such choices possible.

Democracy is not divinely ordained. It is not the natural and inevitable form of government. History teaches us that democracy can perish when not undergirded by moral values. Among these values are equality, tolerance, and loyalty, which focus on democracy's common purposes: the dignity of the individual, human rights, and self–government. Take away any of these three moral values and a crisis of confidence in democracy will follow. Such a crisis may strike at the soul and the spirit of democracy.

I am glad of the opportunity to express my gratitude to my dear friend Mr. Richard Young for his kindness in reading my manuscripts and offering valuable advice.

I also wish to thank Dr. Lawson Taitte for his fruitful assistance in research and Mrs. Mary Hansen for her patience in typing and retyping my manuscript.

Finally, this is also an opportunity to express my gratitude to The University of Texas at Dallas for the honor bestowed upon me in having my name associated with a program designed to deepen the understanding of the importance of moral values in our society. I sincerely hope that the influence of the Lectures on Moral Values in a Free Society named for me and upon which this book is based will be enduringly imprinted on our lives and our society.

CHAPTER 1

EQUALITY

The Idea of Equality

The famous watchwords of the French Revolution—*"Liberté, égalité, fraternité"*—became the rallying cry not only of that revolution itself but of many subsequent generations of liberals and reformers the world over. Among the three ideals of liberty, equality, and brotherhood, the goal of equality has the most complex ramifications in mankind's quest to implement it. Equality has become a byword. The history of mankind can be seen as the history of an increasing passion for equality, and the rise of democratic forms of governance reflects the putting into practice of the operative ideals of liberty and equality.

All men desire to be free and to be respected. This invincible passion for equality can prevail in either of two ways: It can lift the weak up to the level of the strong, or it can drag the strong down to the level of the weak. Poor or disenfranchised people want to be elevated to the rank of the powerful. If they fail in this, their disappointment may induce them to prefer equality in slavery, where rights are given to nobody, to humiliating inequality. Thus it has happened that people's instinctive taste for equality has ignited bloody revolutions that, when they missed their mark, have given birth to emperors and dictators.

A. Greece

The idea of equality has preoccupied the minds of many great thinkers since the ancient philosophers of Greece and Rome and the Hebrew prophets. In Greece, the good life—which was the object of all philosophical inquiry and political activity—was offered only to free individuals. Aristotle, for instance, contemptuously regarded slaves as "living tools." His concept that "equality consists in the same treatment of similar persons" was compatible with the existence of many unequal groups in the Greek polity, where women, aliens, slaves, mechanics, tradesmen, and husbandmen were excluded from the equal possession of liberty enjoyed by free citizens.

In stating that "everywhere inequality is a cause of revolution," Aristotle pointed out that disputes arise "when persons who are not equal receive equal shares." He found the very "springs and fountains of revolution" in the faulty notions concerning equality held by those who advocated democracy and oligarchy. The democrats claimed that since men should be equally free, they should be absolutely equal in all respects. The oligarchs advocated the idea that those who are unequal in one respect are unequal in all respects. The absolute standards that these two forms of government offer, according to Aristotle, "stir up revolution."

In *The Republic*, Plato described the ideal state, to be ruled by philosophers, where private property and family will be abolished and education will fit each for his part in the common life. He was not much interested in equality. In one of his discussions related to the relative equality of the sexes, Plato reached the conclusion that the gifts of nature are alike diffused in men and women; therefore all the pursuits of men are the pursuits of women also, "but in all of them a woman is inferior to a man." Aristotle and Plato accepted the class structure in the Greek city-state as a perfect social organization written in the eternal and final order of political life.

Pericles, the Athenian statesman and one of the greatest patrons of the arts, advanced democracy in Athens through various steps. Among these was the opening of every office to any citizen. The idea of equality was a part of his political leadership. In the celebrated funeral oration made at the end of the first year of the Peloponnesian War (which began in 431 B.C.), Pericles made a strong appeal to the pride and patriotism of the citizens and stressed the importance of equality as the noblest expression of Athenian democracy:

> "If we look to the laws, they afford equal justice to all in their private differences; if to social standing, advancement in public life falls to reputation for capacity, class consideration not being allowed to interfere with merit; nor again does poverty bar the way—if a man is able to serve the state, he is not hindered by the obscurity of his condition. The freedom which we enjoy in our government extends also to our ordinary life."

Somewhat later in the development of Greek thought, the school of the Stoics, which formulated its philosophy in the third and second centuries B.C., advocated the equality of all human beings. The Stoics identified reason with God, and because of each person's ability to reason, they attributed to each a spark of divinity. Slavery, they argued, rejects or denies this fragment of divinity and therefore should be abolished. In contrast to Aristotle and Plato they stressed the resemblance, rather than the differences, among human beings, as well as the unity of mankind bound by universal law. Under this law, they claimed, all human beings are equal.

B. Rome

The Roman philosophers adopted this stoic conception of natural law. The Roman dramatist and statesman Lucius Annaeus Seneca observed that the "world is the one parent of all." Cicero, the Roman politician and philosopher, pointed out the similarity among all members of the human race by claiming, "And so, however we may define man, a single definition will apply to all." He saw all mankind bound together by feelings of justice and by "kindliness and good-will." The Pax Romana, the Roman peace based on Roman arms, offered the blessing of peace for the great empire from which even the victims of Rome's conquests benefited. The Romans granted some privileges and rights to the conquered, subject peoples, and in A.D. 212 the Emperor Caracalla granted full citizenship to all free inhabitants of Rome, slaves excluded. This universalism was realized, however, only in appearance. Octavian, hailed as the "restorer of the commonwealth and the champion of freedom," who (to quote his own words) "handed over the republic to the control of the senate and the people of Rome," retained in substance the autocratic authority he had resigned. Roman imperialism did not provide the climate in which equality could flourish.

C. The Old and New Testaments

To the Hebrews, in spite of the dissimilarities among human beings, the Lord is the maker of all men, the rich and the poor. (Prov. 22:2.) In relation to God, all men are equal and all have to fulfill His purposes and to perform His will in return for His mercy. Job, referring to his servant, asks: "Did not he that made me in the womb, make him?" (31:15.) The Psalmist proclaims that "the Lord looked from heaven; he beholdeth all the sons of men." (33:13.) Prophetic judgment is leveled at those "which oppress the poor, which crush the needy" (Amos 4:1) and those who "swallow up the needy, even to make the poor of the land to fail." (Amos 8:4.)

The prophet Amos, disturbed by the voices of those who regarded Israel as a chosen nation and as a special servant of God among the nations, cries out in the name of the Lord, "Are you not as the children of the Ethiopians unto me, O children of Israel? saith the Lord. Have not I brought up Israel out of the Land of Egypt? and the Philistines from Caphtor, and the Syrians from Kir?" (Amos 9:7.)

These attitudes are further developed in the New Testament. The idea of equality is extended by Jesus in stressing the need to serve one's fellowman.

"Whoever wants to be great must be your servant, and whoever wants to be first must be the willing slave of all." (Mark 10:43.) Although Jesus' teaching transcended all social, political, and economic circumstances, the moral discrimination between the powerful and the weak, between the rich and the poor, is maintained in the New Testament, beginning with Mary's *Magnificat:* "He has torn imperial powers from their thrones, but the humble have been lifted high. The hungry he has satisfied with good things, the rich sent empty away." Jesus' blessing upon the poor and His woes upon the rich, as recorded in the Beatitudes in Luke, maintain the same moral discrimination and concern for the weak and the oppressed.

Christianity extended the concept of equality to all. The chosen people of Israel are not the only children of God, since, as Paul explained in his letter to the Galatians, "there is no such thing as Jew and Greek, slave and freeman, male and female; for you are all one person in Christ Jesus." (3:28.) The same message of the universal nature of equality is repeated in Paul's letter to the Colossians (3:10) and by Peter, who at the invitation of the gentile Cornelius addressed a large gathering: "I now see how true it is that God has no favorites, but that in every nation the man who is godfearing and does what is right is acceptable to him." (Acts 10:34.)

D. The Feudal Society of the Middle Ages

In the Middle Ages, the feudal social organization typical of all Western Europe was based on a strict

class division into three main categories, the nobility, the clergy, and the peasants. The church reflected this feudal organization and accepted its social
stratification. Its hierarchy somewhat paralleled the
feudal hierarchy of nobles. The church owned much
land, which was held in the hands of the monasteries,
the churches themselves, and the church dignitaries,
who lived in splendor much like that of the powerful nobles, while some of the priests lived in base
poverty. By association with the civil power, the
church expanded its influence and grew rich through
gifts and bequests given by pious nobles.

Although such figures as Saint Francis of Assisi
carried out vows of poverty, the disruptive forces of
deep inequality that were present in the feudal system also divided the church itself. As adapted to the
medieval feudal society, the church, full of abuses,
especially in the management of its great ecclesiastical properties, was not interested in seeking human
equality nor in accepting it as one of the supreme
values for which the church was established. The
church used Saint Augustine's idea about God's
saving grace as the first step toward salvation (later
developed by Calvin and the Jansenists in their
predestination theologies) to interpret and to justify
worldly inequalities and sufferings.

Starting in the fourteenth century, there were
movements for ecclesiastical reform, such as those
launched by the Lollards and the Anabaptists. The
Lollards, led by John Wycliffe (whose books were
ordered burned by a papal bill in 1410), claimed that
the clergy by becoming rich had abandoned the
church's mission. In contrast, they spread the idea

of the establishment of evangelical poverty. The Anabaptists (distinguished from the Baptists) also advocated far-reaching social and economic reforms. Their social views were determined by their belief in the equality that should reign in absolute brotherhood in Christ.

E. The Protestant Reformation

Martin Luther, the leader of the Protestant Reformation, sought to suppress the Anabaptist movement, which was one of the factors of the Peasant War of 1524–1525. Luther, who drew a sharp line between political and spiritual jurisdiction, condemned the peasants' uprising against serfdom as a revolt against civil authority. Luther's conviction that a society should have unequal classes, that "some are free, others captives, some masters, others subjects," and his distrust of merchants and peasants relate to the economic conditions of the sixteenth century. Yet, in spiritual life, Luther in a very real sense stressed equality.

Luther revolted, not against the church, but against the corruption and exploitation of the church by the Papacy, against the church as an empire. He denounced monopolies, describing those who establish them as "not worthy to be called human beings . . . for their envy and avarice are so coarse and shameless. . . ." He preached passionately against usury and extortioners. Although he accepted the existing social hierarchy with its institution of serfdom as a necessary foundation of society, he vindicated the spiritual freedom of the individual.

God, according to Luther, speaks as a voice in the heart of each individual and not through the mediation of the priesthood. He advocated that the canon law should therefore be abolished. It is intolerable, he wrote, "that in canon law so much importance is attached to the freedom, life, [and] property of the clergy. . . . If a priest is killed, the land is laid under interdict—why not when a peasant is killed? Whence comes this great distinction between those who are equally Christian?"

Calvinism differs theologically from Lutheranism chiefly in the doctrine of predestination. (To many, Calvinism is synonymous with predestination.) John Calvin, the French Protestant Reformer, insisted more than Luther on the doctrine of an eternal decree of God that out of free grace saves some people, but not others. This decision of whom to elect is predestination to salvation. Therefore, Calvin maintained that "all are not created on equal terms, but some are preordained to eternal life, others to eternal damnation." Among the "preordained" to be saved, there is no distinction of persons—all are equal in the sight of God. Calvin's idea of social reconstruction through the supervision of the church denied the existing hierarchy of offices. God's commandment to the individual to work for the divine glory, according to Calvin, calls for the avoidance of all spontaneous enjoyment of life without distinction of rank or wealth.

F. The Levellers and the Diggers

Lutheranism and Calvinism greatly influenced the

Puritan Revolution in England. In the seventeenth century the Levellers, an English politico-religious movement, aimed at religious and political equality (the term Levellers was pejorative, because of their purpose of making all men "level" to fulfill the prophecy of Isaiah 40:4). Their leader, John Lilburne (1614–1657), in his pamphlet *The Free Man's Freedom Vindicated* found "it unnatural, irrational, sinful, wicked, unjust, devilish, and tyrannical. . . . for any man whatsoever, spiritual or temporal, clergyman or layman, to appropriate and assume unto himself, a power, authority, and jurisdiction, to rule, govern, or reign over any sort of men in the world without their free consent. . . ." The Levellers argued that the authority of the state should rest upon an Agreement of the People, drafted by the representatives of the rank and file in Cromwell's army. Under such an agreement, the authority of the republic should be vested in one representative house elected once each two years by full manhood suffrage.

The Levellers' concept of equality was explained by Colonel Rainborough in the Putney debate of 1647 between the officers and the soldiers of Cromwell's army:

> "For really I think that the poorest he that is in England hath a life to live, as the greatest he; and therefore truly, sir, I think it's clear, that every man that is to live under a government ought first by his own consent to put himself under that government; and I do think that the poorest man in England is not at all bound in a strict sense to

that government that he hath not had a voice to put himself under."

While the Levellers made a contribution to the development of the idea of political equality, a small left-wing group of the Levellers known as the Diggers stressed the interdependence of political and economic equality. Their leader, Gerrard Winstanley, in his pamphlet *The Law of Freedom in a Platform*, pointed out that economic conditions are the root of tyranny. There is no need, he wrote, for one person to be richer than another, "for Riches make men vainglorious, proud, and to oppress their Brethren; and are occasion of wars." The Diggers believed that "common land" should be distributed among the poor to cultivate.

"The State of Nature"

A. Spinoza

During the remainder of the seventeenth century, the idea of equality dominated the thought of prominent philosophers, such as Spinoza, Hobbes, and Locke. In his *Theologico-Political Treatise*, Spinoza stated that the best life is secured in democracy, which he defined as "a society which wields all its power as a whole." Of all forms of government he saw democracy

"as the most natural and the most consonant with individual liberty. In it no one transfers his natural right so absolutely that he has no further voice in affairs; he only hands it over to the majority of a society of which he is a unit. Thus all men remain equals, as they were in the state of nature."

Spinoza saw perils in "the state of nature," in which "everyone did everything he liked and reason's claim was lowered to a par with those of hatred and anger." To avoid these perils, Spinoza maintained, individuals by social compact hand over their natural rights to the sovereign power. The sovereign has the right to impose "any commands he pleases," and it is through the laws he enacts that justice and injustice arise.

B. Hobbes

The perils of the state of nature were also stressed by the English philosopher Thomas Hobbes, the author of *Leviathan*, one of the most prominent political treatises in European literature in the seventeenth century. According to Hobbes, men are by nature equal in bodily and mental capabilities. Because of this natural equality, men seek and pursue their own conservation and have equal hopes of attaining the ends to which they are naturally impelled. In the nature of man, stated Hobbes, we find three principal causes that lead to a state of war with one another: competition, mistrust, and a desire for glory. In this state of war, "force and fraud" are the "cardinal virtues"; the individual is dependent on his own strength for his security, and "the notions of

right and wrong, justice and injustice, have no place."
Only through the organization of society and the
establishment of a commonwealth can peace be
obtained.

C. Locke

The English philosopher John Locke, on the other
hand, saw a radical difference between the state of
nature and the state of war. He rejected completely
Hobbes's concept of the state of nature. In Locke's
view "all men are naturally in that state and remain
so till by their own consent they make themselves
members of some political society." Force, exercised
without right, constitutes a violation of the state of
nature. The proper state of nature is where people
live together "according to reason, without a common superior on earth with authority to judge
between them. . . ." For Hobbes, natural law meant
power, fraud, and force. For Locke, natural law
meant the universally accepted moral law promul-
gated by human reason as it reflects on God and on
man's relation to God. This relation calls for the
fundamental equality of all men as rational creatures
endowed with reason.

The principal new thoughts during the Enlightenment about the right to liberty and equality can be
traced to Locke and to his assertion that a man enters
this world not already equipped with ideas but with
a mind that is a *tabula rasa*, blank and ready to be
shaped by experience. According to Locke, the
natural moral law is discoverable by reason, and the
state of nature is the state of liberty. "The state of

nature," he taught, "has a law of nature to govern, which obliges every one; and reason, which is that law, teaches all mankind. . . . that, being all equal and independent, no one ought to harm another in his life, health, liberty, or possessions." Thus Locke's theory of intellectual development implied the rejection of the basis of traditional hereditary inequalities.

Men, stated Locke, were endowed with certain natural rights even before there was a state. He based his exposition of individual liberty and equality on natural law and on his idea of a social contract arrived at by people in building their society. This social contract theory argues that sovereignty resides in the people, who have the moral right to overthrow a government that does not reflect the popular will.

D. Rousseau

The state of nature was also widely discussed by Jean Jacques Rousseau, the most frequently quoted thinker of eighteenth-century France. He has been praised as a prominent philosopher and ridiculed as an eccentric; he has been studied seriously as an influential theorist of his time and rebuffed for his lack of historical perspective and for deficiencies in his knowledge of history. His first major publication, the *Discourse on the Arts and Sciences*, which made him suddenly famous, was written in response to a contest offered by the Academy of Dijon for the best answer to the question, "Has the progress of the arts and sciences tended to the purification or the corruption of morality?" In the prize-winning essay, published in 1750, Rousseau gave a defiantly negative answer. As a popularizer of the idea of the "noble savage," he distrusted the idea of progress.

The myth of a natural man uncorrupted by the advances of civilization was so enticing to Rousseau that he could see only corruption in the advent of new development in the arts and sciences. In the second part of the *Discourse*, he stated, "Astronomy was born from superstition, eloquence from ambition, hate, flattery and falsehood; geometry from avarice; physics from vain curiosity; all, even moral philosophy, from human pride. Thus the sciences and arts owe their birth to our vices." (Translated by Roger D. and Judith R. Masters, St. Martin's Press, 1964, p. 48.)

Rousseau tried to support this thesis by references to history. When the Goths ravaged Greece, he wrote, they saved the libraries from burning in order to turn the enemies away from military exercise "and amuse them with idle and sedentary occupations." The military virtue of Romans died, he argued, when they "became connoisseurs of paintings, engravings, [and] jeweled vessels, and began to cultivate the fine arts." The most evident effect and the most dangerous consequence of the arts and sciences, concluded Rousseau, is "the disastrous inequality introduced among men by the destruction of talents and the debasement of virtues."

Five years later the Academy of Dijon also offered a prize for the best essay on the question, "What is the origin of inequality among men and is it in accordance with the natural law?" Rousseau's *Discourse on the Origin and Foundations of Inequality Among Men* did not win the prize, but it was published in 1758.

The greatest social interest of men in a society is, according to this *Discourse*, the inhibition of inequality. The worst of all social evils is thus institutional inequality. Rousseau argued that man living outside society was "wandering up and down the forests without industry, without speech and without home, an equal stranger to war and to all ties, neither standing in need of his fellow-creatures nor having any desire to hurt them." His fundamental impulse was self-love in the sense of the impulse of self-preservation. When he took note of his fellows, a second impulse of compassion came into operation.

In the pure state of nature all men had been equal. When they found their existence threatened by violence and war, they concluded a social contract that led to a political community that would judge conflicts between individuals and regulate "the choice and power of magistrates" charged with enforcement of law and order. It also led to the transformation of mere possession into a lawful right to property in which Rousseau saw the cause "of crimes, wars, murders, miseries, and horrors."

The idea of the equality of the natural man undergirds Rousseau's theory of the General Will. It may be mentioned that he did not invent the phrase "general will," but he determined its history. It was Montesquieu who saw in legislative power the "general will *(volunté general)* of the state," while the role of the executive power was the execution of the general will. Unlike Montesquieu, Rousseau refused to accept the sort of civil liberty that existed only among the aristocrats in the Europe of his day. It is wrong, he wrote, that "the privileged few should gorge themselves with superfluities while the starving multitude is in want of the base necessities of life."

Rousseau, at one time closely associated with Denis Diderot, also rejected Diderot's notion of the general will as the universal bond obliging mankind. The belief in progress and enlightenment, emphasized in Diderot's *Encyclopedia*, was challenged by Rousseau in his aforementioned view that the arts and sciences have a corrupting influence on equality and are unrelated to true virtue. The general will, argued Rousseau, is the voice of the people, in fact the voice of God *(vox populi, vox dei)*. The important role of a legitimate and popular government is "to follow in everything the general will," and the "first duty of the legislator is to make the laws conformable to the general will."

Rousseau's state of nature was, not the state of "war of all against all" *(homo homini lupus)* that Hobbes described, but a state of egalitarian independence. Like a peaceful animal, primitive man was "satisfying his hunger at the first oak and slaking his thirst at the first brook, finding his bed at the foot of the tree which afforded him a repast; and with that, all his wants [were] supplied." The rise of moral and political inequality, according to Rousseau, should be attributed to the establishment of private property, to the improvement of human faculties, and to the establishment of political society, government, and law. In his account of the origin of inequality, Rousseau saw three stages: The first stage was the establishment of the law and of the right of property, the second was the institution of government, and the third and last "was the changing of legitimate power into arbitrary power."

Rousseau was right in describing tyrannical rule as "the last stage of inequality." A full circle takes place when we arrive at despotism. Men return to their first equality when the tyrant reduces them to slaves. Then inequality becomes the equality of slaves. All Rousseau's other conclusions, however, can hardly be applied to modern society. His ideal political system was that of a small city-state in which the body of patriotic citizens is sovereign and the citizens in a straightforward, democratic manner vote in a popular assembly. In large states such assemblies are impracticable.

Furthermore, the *First Discourse* and the *Second Discourse* are full of contradictions and paradoxes. Rousseau loathed scholars and intellectuals generally, yet he wrote his discourses for the learned Academy of Dijon. He himself acknowledged this contradiction by asking, "How can one dare blame the sciences before one of Europe's most learned societies, praise ignorance in a famous Academy, and reconcile contempt for study with respect for the truly learned?" Many of his other writings also have a paradoxical character. In the book *Emile*, Rousseau admitted, "Common readers, pardon my paradoxes; they must be made when one thinks seriously; and, whatever you may say, I would rather be a man of paradoxes than a man of prejudices." But the reduction of the natural man to a peaceful but unthinking animal is not a matter of prejudices. It is a paradox of such a pernicious sort that it prompted Voltaire to call the *Discourse on Inequality* a "book against the human race."

Equality as a Vehicle of Vindictiveness

As discussed above, the view of human equality emphasized in the Old and New Testaments—as well as the view of many subsequent religious leaders and philosophers—concentrated on the arrogance of the rich and powerful and the humility of the poor. But do the poor and humble retain their humility when they cease to be poor and themselves become the wielders of power? The passion for equality can turn into a vehicle of vindictiveness when those who seek equality, upon gaining power, exhibit the same arrogance and cruelty that they abhorred in their oppressors. The French and Bolshevik revolutions give vivid illustrations of what happens when the fortunes of events transmute the weakness of the oppressed into strength and desire for power.

A. The French Revolution

In France at the end of the eighteenth century, the tension caused by the deep-seated discontent of the unprivileged lower classes became intolerable. The privileges of the nobles and of the clergy became onerous burdens on the peasants, the working classes, and the bourgeoisie. The middle class, or bourgeoisie, built up by the expansion of commerce and the growing popularity of the laissez-faire doctrine of Adam Smith, clamored for power. Three estates formed the legislative body: The First Estate consisted of the upper clergy; the Second Estate, of nobles; and the Third Estate, of the lower clergy, the bourgeoisie, and artisans. This theoretical representation did little for the lower orders, however. The heavily taxed lower classes could not exert any power, because the king refused to convoke the legislature.

The Paris mob, discontented because of the prevailing misrule, disorder, corruption, and financial chaos, revolted and on July 14, 1789, stormed and destroyed the prison of the Bastille. The insurrection spread rapidly throughout France. Chateaus belonging to nobility were burned, the owners murdered or driven away, tax collectors assaulted. Headed by Jean Paul Marat, the radical Commune of Paris, which replaced the Paris government, and the radical Jacobins, with Robespierre as their leader, were blinded by the extreme idea of "liberty and equality" and were responsible for the September Massacres of 1792, when thousands of aristocrats, priests, and others suspected of hostility to the revolution were murdered.

During the same month, the monarchy was abolished and the First Republic established. Louis XVI, convicted of treason, was guillotined in January of 1793. The Revolutionary Tribunal went to work, and the Reign of Terror began. Opulence was proclaimed "infamous." To obtain equality, the rulers taxed property and confiscated it to be divided among the poor. The guillotine became the official instrument of execution, and it chopped off heads day after day, week after week. The struggle for power among various groups resulted in an incredible butchery. The victims of the mass slaughtering included Marat and Georges Jacques Danton, leaving

Robespierre the master of the revolution until he himself was executed on 9 Thermidor (July 27, 1794).

The Great Terror brought the Thermidorian reaction. France, weary of blood, stress, and confusion, was ready to abandon the extreme of revolution. After a series of insurrections, stalemates, and coups d'etat, "New France" was ready to take on some likeness of the old, to accept Napoleon as its ruler, and to endure an emperor.

B. The Bolshevik Revolution

A parallel process to that of the rise of terror during the first French Revolution took place in Russia early in this century. The disintegration of the autocratic government of the Romanov dynasty led to the abdication of Nicholas II on March 15, 1917. The disorganization of the country that had followed the defeats suffered during World War I was extreme. With the army in a state of mutiny, the slogans of equality, liberty, and unity offered by the Bolsheviks were very appealing to the hundreds of thousands of soldiers wandering back from the war zone to their homes. The Bolsheviks' well-established tradition of terrorism and opportunism encouraged the peasants and the workers to satisfy their demands by direct action. They rose against the landowners, burned chateaus, looted houses, and robbed and murdered innocent men and women.

The election on November 17, 1917, of a Constituent Assembly produced only a 24 percent vote for the Bolsheviks. The Bolshevik-led troops, having arrested a number of the elected delegates, surrounded Petrograd's Tauride Palace, in which the Constituent Assembly met; dissolved the assembly; and moved on to establish throughout the country a one-party dictatorship. The Politburo, composed of seven members, became the governing body of the party and of Russia as well.

The changes in economic life introduced by the communists during the first three years of their regime were no less revolutionary than the changes made in Russia's political system. The results of the implementation of the fundamental concept of their economic thought—equality and justice to be obtained through preventing the capitalists and the landlords from exploiting the workers and the peasants—remind us of the observation made by the early-twentieth-century philosopher Ortega y Gasset, who said, "The mob goes in search of bread, and the means it employs is generally to wreck bakeries."

The economic system envisaged by the communist leaders called for the nationalization of all means of production, transportation, trade, and banking and of all land, forests, and minerals. In the process of the punitive nationalization of all kinds of industries, the responsibility of management was vested in workers who were not prepared by education or training. The resulting failure to coordinate the supply of raw materials, transportation, and distribution caused chaos and a collapse of industry that proved to be disastrous to Russia's economic life.

In the realm of agriculture the Soviet government seized grain by force when the peasants resorted to passive resistance against the food dictatorship established in May 1918. The peasants, who were bearing the principal burden of the cost of industrialization, had to turn over to the state all grain above the minimum needed for consumption by their families and for seed. The peasants resisted vigorously the establishment of a state monopoly in grain, and a great deal of bloodshed occurred. As a result of the reduced food supply and of the severe famine, many died from starvation.

Having antagonized the great body of the proletariat and of the peasants, the communists were forced to make concessions and to retreat by inaugurating a New Economic Policy (NEP). The NEP permitted peasants to rent land for limited periods of time and allowed small factories and shops to employ a certain number of wage laborers. A fixed tax was substituted for the system of requisitioning grain from the peasants, who were allowed to retain and dispose of freely in the open market whatever they produced over and above the amount of the imposed tax. Establishments engaged in small industry and domestic trade were restored to private enterprise. The NEP inaugurated a period of economic convalescence at a considerable sacrifice of socialist principles. The compromises made by the communists were, however, of only a temporary nature. The substance of Karl Marx's program was the nationalization of the means of production, and that program was still at the heart of Soviet intentions.

With the adoption of the 1928 Five-Year Plan, the concessions to private initiative were annulled or severely restricted. The communist party was also undergoing a great upheaval, reflecting the bitter conflict that had been going on within its own ranks.

As in the French Revolution, the leader who gained all the power rid himself of his rivals by a recourse to treason trials. Of the seven members of the 1920 Politburo, six were purged by Joseph Stalin. Following the great purge trials of 1935–1938, with their sensational confessions, those who were opposed to the Stalin regime or who voiced their discontent were liquidated by firing squad.

In agriculture the collectivization of holdings of the prosperous peasants, called kulaks, proceeded for the sake of "equality." Their houses, livestock, and tools were confiscated, and they were banished to remote concentration camps where they were compelled to furnish unpaid labor without being provided even the minimum goods needed to survive.

The Soviet secret police (the NKVD, presently the KGB) became the largest employer of labor in the nation. In the concentration camps scattered all over the country, the kulaks were joined by political opponents, members of minority groups, and others sentenced to hard labor for often-imaginary offenses. In the nation's economic planning, the secret police were responsible for carrying out a considerable segment of the capital construction planned. One of the purposes of mass arrests was thus to supply forced unpaid labor. The work to be done by forced labor included mining, producing timber, and building railroads, canals, tunnels, highways, and military camps. It was estimated that by 1940, during Stalin's time, the number of prisoners rose to perhaps as many as 20 million.

The passion for equality, as we mentioned, can

turn into a vehicle of brutality for brutality's sake. Robespierre, guided by a consuming passion for a new order of life, saw himself surrounded by wicked men, whom, in defense of humanity, he had sent to the guillotine. Stalin's repression was designed to instill fear—it often bore no relevance to the stated purposes of the communist state, which included the objective of equality. He destroyed and killed out of vindictiveness, meanness, and paranoia.

The Dangers in the Passion for Equality

The experience of the French Revolution undoubtedly prompted Alexis de Tocqueville to observe the dangers that occur when the passions engendered by the idea of equality turn violent:

> "Democratic peoples always like equality, but there are times when their passion for it turns to delirium. This happens when the old social hierarchy, long menaced, finally collapses after a severe internal struggle and the barriers of rank are at length thrown down. At such times men pounce on equality as their booty and cling to it as a precious treasure they fear to have snatched away. The passion for equality seeps into every corner of the human heart, expands, and fills the whole. It is no use telling them that by this blind surrender to an exclusive passion they are compromising their dearest interests; they are deaf. It is no use pointing out that freedom is slipping from their grasp while they look the other way; they are blind, or rather they can see but one

thing to covet in the whole world." (*Democracy in America*, a new translation by George Lawrence, 1966, Harper & Row, p. 475.)

It may be noted that Tocqueville thought of calling the second volume of his book *L'Egalité en Amerique* but changed the word "equality" to "democracy." Perhaps the reason for this decision was the experience of the French Revolution, which demonstrated that equality is not always a manifestation of freedom, or perhaps it was that the term "democracy" used by the Americans in President Andrew Jackson's day, when Tocqueville visited the United States, was more entrenched there and elsewhere. Tocqueville uses the term "democracy" to refer to the United States in the broadest terms. It includes the equality proclaimed in the very beginning of American history as the leading feature of the country. The unfailing faith of the American settlers that equality of conditions signifies freedom from being ruled and from ruling others prompted Tocqueville to write in his Introduction:

"No novelty in the United States struck me more vividly during my stay there than the equality of conditions. It was easy to see the immense influence of this basic fact on the whole course of society. It gives a particular turn to public opinion and a particular twist to the laws, new maxims to those who govern and particular habits to the governed.

"I soon realized that the influence of this fact extends far beyond political government; it creates opinions, gives birth to feelings, suggests customs, and modifies whatever it does not create.

"So the more I studied American society, the more clearly I saw equality of conditions as the creative element from which each particular fact derived, and all my observations constantly returned to this nodal point." (*Ibid.*, p. 3.)

It is noteworthy that Tocqueville repeatedly stressed that in the contest for freedom and equality, people want both, but if they cannot have freedom, "they still want equality in slavery." (*Ibid.*, p. 475.) In Chapter 1 of Volume II, Part II, of *Democracy in America*, which he entitled "Why Democratic Nations Show a More Ardent and Enduring Love for Equality than for Liberty," he explained that equality, not freedom, is the chief and continued object of mankind's desires. People, he wrote, seek freedom with "quick and sudden impulses," but if they fail to obtain it, "they resign themselves to their disappointment; but nothing will satisfy them without equality, and they would rather die than lose it." (*Ibid.*, p. 49.)

In the light of Tocqueville's observations that his contemporaries loved equality more tenaciously than liberty, how can we explain his classical account of American equality in freedom, quoted above, which implies that there is an organic relationship between equality and freedom, rather than a contest between them? How did the "equality of conditions" in the United States differ from the political experiences of other nations? What was the distinctive character of the new environment at the beginning of American history in which equality in freedom was expected to flourish.

Equality in Freedom

We can find one of the answers to these questions in the fact that the United States was the only nation aware, before it came into existence, of the purpose of equality in freedom. In other nations, in Tocqueville's time, revolutions for the sake of equality erupted as a reaction against corruption, abuse, brutality, and exploitation. When the revolution succeeded in overthrowing the ruling government, the masters of the revolution took the place of the oppressors. A mass of citizens confused about their rights and duties fell easily under the yoke of new rulers, who often proved to be more barbaric than the governments that collapsed.

The settlers of the United States did not come here to establish political dominion over others. They came, not to rehabilitate an ancient organization of society by giving it an improved form, but to start a new nation with a new purpose—a project which had never been tried before. This new historic process started long before the American Revolution. As John Adams wrote to a Dr. Mise on January 1, 1816, the war for independence was "not a revolutionary war, for the revolution was complete, in the minds of the people, and the union of the colonies, before the war commenced in the skirmishes of Concord and Lexington on the 19th of April 1775."

The Pilgrims of the *Mayflower* left an old society behind them, and they had no intention of accepting its principles as a pattern for the new society they were determined to build. The society they founded had a radically different purpose from those of existing societies. This purpose was equality in freedom—a freedom that offered each man the opportunity to rise as high as merit would carry him. This was the reason for our nation's existence as an independent entity. The Founding Fathers, in the Declaration of Independence, set forth this purpose of personal equality in freedom as a fundamental tenet of this nation's political faith.

Equality of Opportunity—Economic Equality

We can find another answer to the questions posed above in the distinctive American concept of equality, which differed dramatically from the deeply rooted tradition of social hierarchy in Europe, where a person's principal distinguishing quality was his birth and where the rich and the poor were far removed from each other socially as well as economically. The American ideal of equality focused on the opportunity for each citizen to make his own place in the society, with none excluded by birth from access to political rule. Describing contemporary society in the United States in his *Letters from an American Farmer*, the American author J. Hector St. John (1735–1813) wrote:

"It is not composed, as in Europe, of great lords who possess everything, and of herds of people who have nothing. There are no aristocratical families, no courts, no kings, no bishops, no ecclesiastical dominion, no invisible power giving to a few a very visible one; no great manufacturers employing thousands, no great refinement of luxury. . . . We have no princes for whom we toil, starve and bleed; we are the most perfect society now existing in the world. Here man is free as he ought to be; nor is this pleasing equality so transitory as many others are."

In the same spirit, Benjamin Franklin, the statesman and scientist who was the first American to become widely known abroad, advised those "who would remove to America" about the new American society: "There are few great proprietors of the soil, and few tenants; most people cultivate their own lands, or follow some handicraft or merchandise; very few [are] rich enough to live idly upon their rents or incomes. . . ." The would-be immigrants to America, he wrote, should therefore expect a different world from the one they lived in in Europe, since they would find in the United States "few people so miserable as the poor of Europe" and also "very few that in Europe would be called rich[;] it is rather a general happy mediocrity that prevails."

It should also be noted that the American concept of equality in freedom differed in substance from the equality espoused by the French Revolution or the Marxists. The European egalitarianism advocated that all men should occupy a uniform position on a common level in wealth, income, and power. The American idea of equality stressed equality in opportunity, which can lift men from rags to riches, from the log cabin to the White House, and put strong emphasis upon freedom as the means to make equality a reality. It asserted unalienable birthrights of everybody in all areas of life. Individual status depended not upon inherited but upon achieved qualities. Benjamin Franklin expressed this explicitly when he said that in America people "do not inquire concerning a stranger: *What is he?* but *What can he do?*"

American equality did not demand equality of wealth and income or advocate the confiscation of property and its division among the poor and home-less. Abraham Lincoln advised, "Let not him who is houseless pull down the house of another, but let him work diligently and build one for himself, thus by example assuring that his home should be safe from violence when built."

To answer the question of what the distinctive character of the environment at the beginning of American history was that gave hopes for equality in freedom to flourish, we find the Charter of James I of 1620, which says:

> "[T]he appointed time is come in which Almighty God in his great goodness and bounty. . . . has thought fit and determined, that those large and goodly territories, deserted as it were by their natural inhabitants, should be possessed and enjoyed by such of our subjects and people as heretofore have and hereafter shall by his mercy and favor. . . ."

Four million people, poor but with the potentiality of acquiring limitless wealth, were scattered over a vast area. The settlers, rich in land and released from the institutions that had evolved in Europe in the past, planned the United States as a country where the idea of equality in freedom would stand out very prominently. This idea could be realized only in the kind of environment described by John Adams:

> "In the present state of society and manners in America, with a people living chiefly by agriculture, in small numbers, sprinkled over large tracts of land, they are not subject to those panics and transports, those contagions of madness and folly, which are seen in countries where large numbers live in small places, in daily fear of perishing for want. We know, therefore, that the people can live and increase under almost any kind of government, or without any government at all."

The early settler, compared by John Locke to a "king of a large and fruitful territory" but "clad worse than a day-labourer in England," sought a political equality that would provide him an effective share in the policy decisions that would shape the life of the community in which he lived. The empty spaces of fertile land meant that he had, not only equality of opportunity to provide for his material needs and to secure the good things of life, but the conditions in which the opportunity could exist. In the vast territories he did not find the social barriers and the irrational social discrimination of the "old society." His right to belong to associations of his choice and to participate in group life, although "sprinkled over large tracts of land," provided him with civil and legal equality.

"The Great American Experiment"

The faith of the founders of the United States that the Creator has endowed all human beings with the right to be free and to have equal opportunity endowed our nation with a sense of mission that was expressed in the opening paragraph of *The Federalist* papers. By our "conduct and example," it was said, our people hoped to demonstrate to all the world the advantage of a free and self-governing society. This mission became known as the "great American experiment."

The equalization of opportunity in political, economic, religious, and social life became known as the "American dream." The hope that this great American experiment would serve as an example for other nations to emulate was also expressed by Abraham Lincoln, who asserted that the Declaration of Independence gave "liberty, not alone to the people of this country, but hope to the world for all future time." It gave "promise that in due time the weights should be lifted from the shoulders of all men. . . ." All the world looked on to see whether the American dream would materialize.

This dream, however, has never been fully realized. There was a serious gap between the ideals and the practices of the American republic. What was the cause of this gap? We may also ask why the dream never ceased to inspire this nation to raise its voice on behalf of equal opportunities for jobs, homes, education, and good health. Why does the United States remain the only hope of the oppressed everywhere? What is the magnetic power this country has to attract men and women of all races and religions, all colors and creeds, to come here to escape tyranny and discrimination?

Slavery and the "Three Compromises"

To answer these questions, we should start with the admission that throughout our history there have been flagrant violations utterly contrary to the idea of equality in freedom. Slavery was one of the most significant obstacles standing in the way of the fulfillment of the American dream. Slavery, having begun with the enslavement of Indians for work in plantations and mines, had been an American institution for over a century and a half before the War of Independence. Historians tell us that 1620, when the Pilgrim Fathers landed in Plymouth in New England, was also the year when a Dutch sloop disembarked the first cargo of Negroes at Jamestown in Virginia. The Negroes toiled under the whip of the overseer when Thomas Jefferson penned the Declaration of Independence, which spoke of self-evident truths, the foremost of which was that each and every individual is endowed by our Creator with "certain unalienable rights—and that among them are Life, Liberty, and the Pursuit of Happiness."

In 1795, Thomas Paine wrote in the "Dissertation on First Principles" that "the principle of equality of rights is clear and simple. Every man can understand it, and it is by understanding his rights that he learns his duties; for where the rights of man are equal, every man finally sees the necessity of protecting the rights of others as the most effectual security of his own." But this principle was not quite "simple" since it did not include blacks, native Americans, or women. Hardly could "every man" be said to understand this principle since the provisions of the unamended Constitution written in 1787 included the famous "three compromises" that have been called the source of the Civil War fought three-quarters of a century later.

The word "slavery" does not appear in the Constitution until we reach the Thirteenth Amendment, adopted after the Civil War. Such circumlocutions as a "person held to service or labor" or "such persons as any of the States now existing shall think proper to admit" are used to avoid the word "slave." The first of the three compromises we find in the famous "three-fifths" clause, Clause 3 of Article I, Section 2. It refers to the apportionment of taxes among the states, "according to their respective Numbers, which shall be determined by adding to the whole number of free persons, including those bound to service for a term of years, and excluding Indians not taxed, three-fifths of all other persons."

Thus three-fifths of the slaves were counted in laying taxes and in ascertaining how many members a state should have in the House of Representatives. The northern states claimed that slave-holding states would be undertaxed by not counting the slaves as population. The South claimed that those states would be overtaxed by counting the slaves. Furthermore, since the number of representatives from any state would be apportioned according to its population, slave-state delegates to the Constitutional Convention favored including every slave, although the slaves were not citizens or voters and had no influence on the lawmaking process. Delegates from the nonslave northern states were opposed to counting slaves. The compromise of equating five black men for three white men that was made for the purposes of taxation was also used to determine representation in the House. By combining the two opposed purposes, direct taxation and representation, a restraint was established that prevented a state from getting too much representation and avoiding the payment of its share of direct taxes.

The second compromise, which we find in Section 9 of Article I, postponed abolition of the slave trade for twenty years (until 1808). The third compromise respecting slavery, found in Section 2 of Article IV, was designed to assure the slave-holding states that slaves who might flee to northern states would not become free. (In 1772, Lord Mansfield, Chief Justice of the King's Bench, declared in the celebrated case of a black man named Somerset that a slave brought by his master from Virginia to England became free.)

The three compromises, and especially the three-fifths clause, may explain the position of the U. S. Supreme Court in the case of *Dred Scott v. John F. A. Stanford* (19 How. 393–638, 15 L. Ed. 691 [1857]), in which Chief Justice Taney declared that Negroes were a subordinate and "inferior class" of beings and ascribed to the founders of the Constitution the intention to perpetuate the "impassable barrier" between the white race and the whole "enslaved African race" (including mulattoes). The Court further concluded that Negroes are "altogether unfit to associate with the white race, either in social or political relations and so far inferior, that they had no rights which the white man was bound to respect. . . ." (*Ibid.*, p. 407.)

Because of the three compromises, especially the three-fifths clause, some citizens denounced the celebration of the bicentennial honoring the Constitution in 1987. They refused to celebrate a historical document that permitted slavery to continue and that expressed the view that a black is only a fraction of a human being. It may be argued that in the struggle between proslavery and antislavery forces the compromises offered the only chance of a union that would include the South. It may also be argued that Chief Justice Taney was wrong since at the Constitutional Convention the Founders stressed that the principles of the Declaration of Independence would remain the bedrock foundation of the Constitution and, in order to save the union, accepted the continuation of slavery as an unavoidable evil. These arguments would not change the fact that compromises that degrade moral values, the human spirit, and human dignity cannot survive or calm down the voices demanding an end to brutality and exploitation. The so-called compromises did not prevent the bloody Civil War, which was followed by constitutional amendments that expanded our definition of equality to encompass minorities and women.

Setbacks to the Commitment

Even with this expanded definition, our country has not had an unblemished record. Setbacks and controversies arose from actual denial of the moral commitment of the Founding Fathers, who dedicated this country to the purpose of freedom for all. America did not remain faithful to their commitment, nor to the legal commitment of the Constitution. The list of disappointments is too long to deal with other than in the broadest way, and we will merely mention some examples that became a part of the American experience of denial of the American purpose. Among the crippling blows, besides the above-mentioned *Dred Scott* decision that foreshadowed the crisis of the Civil War, was the 1896 U. S. Supreme Court decision *Plessy v. Ferguson,* where the Court adopted the doctrine of "separate but equal" by taking the position that the object of the Fourteenth Amendment was not to abolish distinctions based upon color or to enforce social, as distinguished from political, equality, "or commingling of two races upon terms unsatisfactory to either." The Court suggested that legislatures were powerless to eradicate racial instincts, and "if one race is inferior to the other socially, the Constitution of the United States cannot put them upon the same plane."

The separation of the two races resulted in the establishment of separate schools for each and of separate theaters, hotels, restaurants, and railway carriages. The separate-but-equal doctrine spread to parks, playgrounds, swimming pools, and beaches. Because they were barred from the ballot box, blacks had no political influence to remedy these situations. This doctrine lasted 58 years, until the historical unanimous ruling of the U. S. Supreme Court of May 17, 1954, in *Brown v. Board of Education of Topeka, Kansas.*

As we have seen, there were deplorable departures from the concept of equality and freedom, but it should be pointed out that whenever there was a blundering reversion to inequality (and there were many of them) the voice of conscience could still be heard calling for adherence to the ideal of equal access to "life, liberty, and the pursuit of happiness." There were shortcomings in the implementation of equality in freedom, but the strong thread of moral purpose that runs through the fabric of American history should never be ignored or underestimated.

As early as 1769, Thomas Jefferson had urged the Assembly in Virginia to emancipate the slaves in the colony. One of Jefferson's accusations against the crown of Great Britain was that any attempt by the colonists to restrain the slave trade had been checked by the greedy proprietary interest of slave traders in the mother country. (The slave traffic, in the words of Lord Darmouth, was "so beneficient to the nation" that the colonies should not be allowed to check or discourage it.)

Thomas Paine, a few weeks after coming to America, in an essay published March 8, 1775, denounced slavery as no less immoral than "murder, robbery, lewdness, and barbarity." Deploring the "wicked and inhuman ways" used by the slave traders—"the desperate wretches" who "enslave men by violence and murder for gain"—he declared, "So much innocent blood have the managers and supporters of this inhuman trade to answer for to the common Lord of all!"

President Lincoln, reacting to the *Dred Scott* decision, argued that "it is not factious, it is even not disrespectful, to treat it as not having yet quite established a settled doctrine for the Country." Since this decision had not been made by the unanimous concurrence of the Justices and had not been affirmed and reaffirmed through a course of years, he stated, it would not be "revolutionary, to not acquiesce in it as a precedent."

Because of the experience of the Civil War, restrictions that would have been impossible before the war were imposed on the states. To remove the legal doubts about the validity of the Emancipation Proclamation (since it was made under the President's war power) and to liberate slaves everywhere in the country, the Thirteenth Amendment was adopted. It provides that neither slavery nor involuntary servitude shall exist within the United States or any place subject to its jurisdiction. In practice the Thirteenth Amendment was found to be insufficient. The Supreme Court pointed out that in some states the former slaves continued to be forbidden to appear in towns other than as menial servants, that they did not have the right to purchase or own land, that they were not permitted to give testimony in the courts in any case where a white man was a party, and that they were subject to numerous discriminations.

The Equal Protection Clause of the Fourteenth Amendment, adopted July 21, 1868, was primarily written for the liberated blacks, although they are not mentioned in the amendment. The clause was designed to prevent a state from making discriminations between its own citizens because of race, color, or "previous conditions of servitude." (See also the Fifteenth Amendment.) Chief Justice William Howard Taft made a distinction between due process and equal protection when he explained that "the spheres of the protection they offer are not coterminous." Due process, he stated, offers a minimum protection, while equal protection offers a supplemental guarantee. As a supplemental guarantee, the Equal Protection Clause has its own reason for existence and should not be regarded as an incidental right attached to the Due Process Clause. (*Truax v. Corrigan*, 257 U. S. 312, 332, 42 S. Ct. 124, 129 [1921].)

The Voice of National Conscience

The thread of moral purpose, which had always existed but was not always highly visible, came to the surface when Justice John Marshall Harlan in his lone dissent in the case of *Plessy v. Ferguson* wrote:

> "The white race deems itself to be the dominant race in this country, and so it is. . . . But in view of the Constitution, in the eye of the law, there is in this country no superior, dominant ruling class of citizen. There is no class here. Our Constitution is color blind. In respect to civil rights all citizens are equal before the law."

In this century the voice of national conscience became louder. It was heard when President Harry Truman presented to the Congress his 1948 Message on Civil Rights, in which he recommended establishing a permanent Commission on Civil Rights, a Joint Congressional Committee on Civil Rights, and a Civil Rights Division in the Department of Justice; strengthening protection against lynching; providing more adequate protection for the right to vote; establishing a Fair Employment Practice Commission to prevent unfair discrimination in employment; prohibiting discrimination in interstate transportation facilities; and equalizing the opportunities for residents of the United States to become naturalized citizens.

It was President Lyndon B. Johnson who, referring to the Civil Rights Act of 1964, stated:

> "The denial of rights invites increased disorder and violence, and those who would hold back progress toward equality, and at the same time promise racial peace, are deluding themselves and deluding the people. Orderly progress, exact enforcement of law are the only paths to end racial strife."

The Emancipation, declared President Johnson, was a proclamation, not a fact. The compassionate and comprehensive civil rights legislation that passed with the votes of more than two-thirds of the members of both parties of the Congress was a fact, since the laws rightly passed must be observed. (Address delivered before the American Bar Association, New York, N. Y., August 12, 1964.) And again, advocating the Voting Rights Act at Howard University on June 4, 1965, President Johnson called for equality not just "as right and theory but equality as a fact and equality as a result."

Senator Hubert Humphrey, discussing the purpose of Title VI of the Civil Rights Act of 1964, said:

"The bill has a simple purpose. That purpose is to give fellow citizens—Negroes—the same rights and opportunities that white people take for granted. This is no more than what was preached by the prophets, and by Christ Himself. It is no more than what our Constitution guarantees." (110 Cong. Rec. 655 [1964].)

Discrimination Against Women

The purpose of Title VI of the Civil Rights Act is not limited to giving equal rights to Negroes. Through the years women also had not had legal protection against discrimination. English common law did not regard women as legal persons or entities. Since the U. S. Constitution was adopted under the influence of English common law, the decisions of the Supreme Court as late as 1961 did not declare unconstitutional the laws of some states that limited the rights of married women. The discrimination against women consisted in limiting their right to make contracts, have separate domiciles, dispose of property by will, engage in business, exercise the guardianship of children, and participate fully in other important fields of American life.

Women are not mentioned in the Constitution, nor do the words "man," "male," or any other noun or adjective denoting sex occur in the original document. (The Northwest Ordinance, adopted the same year as the Constitution, gave the right to vote and to representation in the general assembly only to "free male inhabitants.") The pronouns used by the Constitution—"he," "himself," and "his"—are as genderless as the nouns "mankind" or, until recently, "chairman." The Fifth Amendment provides that no person shall be compelled in any criminal case to be a witness against himself. There was never any doubt whatsoever that the protection offered by this amendment extends also to women. Although under the Constitution women had equal rights with men, in practice they did not enjoy political equality. The early, largely agricultural American community disregarded women as citizens.

Because the Fourteenth Amendment does not mention women, in the absence of a special guarantee of their rights, the fight for their emancipation continued to grow under the leadership of such courageous reformers as Lucy Stone (1818–1893), Susan Brownell Anthony (1820–1906), Elizabeth Cady Stanton (1815–1902), and others who struggled through all available means to promote the women's suffrage movement. Lucy Stone in 1870 founded the *Woman's Journal*, which was for nearly 50 years the official organ of the National American Suffrage Association. Susan B. Anthony and Elizabeth Stanton secured the first laws in New York guaranteeing women's rights over their children, control of property and wages, and a separate legal existence after marriage. The battle for women's suffrage was won in the United States in 1920 (20 years earlier than in France, 2 years later than in Great Britain and Germany). The Nineteenth Amendment, proclaimed August 20, 1920, rendered ineffective the provisions in many acts of Congress and in many state constitutions that had deprived women of suffrage before this amendment. The fight for equal rights for women has continued throughout the twentieth century.

Civil Rights Legislation

Because the voice of conscience demonstrated that important changes in social values and concerns had occurred, the Equal Protection Clause of the Fourteenth Amendment needed implementation to broaden the scope of protection against discrimination based on race, sex, age, creed, and physical handicap. Executive orders issued by our Presidents to curtail such discrimination lacked adequate means of enforcement. (The first such order was issued by President Franklin D. Roosevelt to create the Fair Employment Practices Commission.) The civil rights legislation of the last two decades—to mention only the Civil Rights Act of 1964 and the Voting Rights Act of 1965, numerous federal regulations and state laws designed to eliminate discrimination, and the current array of legal measures to promote equal employment opportunity—offers more effective and farther-reaching remedies against the barriers of discrimination than does the Equal Protection Clause of the Fourteenth Amendment.

The interpretation of the civil rights legislation by the Supreme Court has established the constitutionality of race-conscious remedial measures. The Court has construed Title VII of the Civil Rights Act of 1964 as requiring the use of racial preferences for the purpose of hiring and advancing those who have been adversely affected by past discriminatory employment practices, even at the expense of other employees innocent of discrimination. Federal regulations also clearly establish that race-conscious action is not only permitted but required to accomplish the remedial objectives of Title VII. The choice of remedies to redress racial discrimination is "a balancing process left, within appropriate constitutional or statutory limits, to the sound discretion of the trial court." (*Franks v. Bowman Transportation Co.*, 424 U. S. 747, 96 S. Ct. [1976].)

The Supreme Court, in a 1987 opinion delivered by Justice William Brennan, took the position that the manifest imbalance reflecting underrepresentation of women and minorities in traditionally segregated jobs allows the employer to adopt an affirmative action plan and take sex or race into account without violating Title VII. For the purpose of remedying such underrepresentation, the employer, stated the Court, did not "trammel the rights of male employees" by promoting a woman over a male employee with a higher test score.

In order to determine whether there is an imbalance reflecting underrepresentation of women and minorities in traditionally segregated job categories, a comparison of the percentage of minorities or women in an employer's work force with the percentage in the area labor market or general population is appropriate for jobs requiring no special expertise or for training programs designed to provide expertise. If a job requires special training, a comparison should be made with the percentage of those in the labor force who possess the relevant qualifications. (*Paul E. Johnson v. Transportation Agency, Santa Clara County, California, et al.*, No. 107 S. Ct. 1444 [1987].)

Justice Antonin Scalia in a dissenting opinion pointed out that the *Johnson* decision effectively replaced the goal of a discrimination-free society with "the quite incompatible goal of proportionate representation by race and by sex in the workplace." There seems to be no consensus whether the elimination of prior discrimination justifies another kind of state-enforced discrimination. Discrimination in reverse is not a solution, because two wrongs do not make a right, but there are no doubts that we have made enormous progress in seeking equality. To realize the extent of this progress we may be reminded of the letter Abigail Adams wrote to her husband, John, at the Continental Congress: "[B]y the way, in the new Code of Laws. . . . I desire you would remember the ladies and be more generous and favorable to them, than were your ancestors. . . . Remember, all men would be tyrants if they could." To which he replied, "Depend upon it, we men know better than to repeal our masculine systems." (*The Book of Abigail and John: Selected Letters of the Adams Family, 1762–1784*, Ed. by L. H. Butterfield, Marc Friedlaender, and Mary-Jo Kline, Harvard University Press, 1975, pp. 121, 123.) The repeal, however, has now taken place in some degree.

Tensions Between Freedom and Equality

Although in the history of our nation there are

pages of racism and discrimination, the voice of national conscience has constantly evoked the image of America as a moral society with a potential for redemption and a desire to remedy anything profoundly wrong. The founders of this nation, with compelling clarity, projected an image of America where not merely some but all people are created with equal rights and where their basic rights are neither conferred by nor derived from the state. This image has the magnetic power that attracts people from all parts of the world to our shores to rejoice in the deep-rooted tradition of the idea that every human being is the heir of the legacy of worthiness left to this world by the Old and New Testaments.

In spite of the sweeping changes in the outlook on equality in our nation, the hope for complete equality in freedom is dimmed by the tension that seems inherently to exist between freedom and equality as a paradoxical condition of democracy. Equality in freedom has a tendency to slip at the moment when we think that democratic institutions are mature enough to grasp it.

The reality of equality in freedom falls short of the dreams which inspired it, primarily because of the confusion about the meaning of freedom and equality in a free society. Glaring hypocrisies result from pushing the ideas of freedom and equality to their extremes. One extreme is the concept of absolute freedom. The other extreme is the egalitarian concept that all people are created equal in every respect, illustrated by the popular appeal of Louisiana Governor Huey Long's slogan of "every man a king." Total freedom is the law of the jungle, where only the fiercest, the strongest, and the most ruthless survive. Freedom is not absolute and is justified only if in pursuing our own interests we do not deprive others of theirs or impede their efforts to obtain it. Regarding equality, much restlessness can be traced to the misguided belief that equal opportunity means equality of success, uniformity, equally distributed rewards, and a guarantee of an absolute equality of results.

By the same token, equality of opportunity does not mean a license for the unrestrained, monopolistic accumulation of wealth. In the field of economics, the concentration of power in the hands of a few is an insidious menace to unfettered competition and an assault upon equal opportunities. Some scholars and jurists, including Justice Louis Brandeis, have spoken of monopolies as "the negation of industrial democracy." The aggregation of capital in the hands of a few individuals or corporations presents, in the words of Justice Harlan, a real danger of "slavery to be fostered on the American people." The accumulation of enormous fortunes is a radical departure from the idea of freedom in which economic and political equality can flourish. It is a half-understood truth, if not irresponsible demagoguery, to maintain that economic centralization leaves open the chance of free trade and competition. In reality, through monopolistic pressures, it eliminates equal competition and escapes the risks to its own privileges that would flow from equal opportunities for the man in the street.

Equality Versus Egalitarianism

No less dangerous than economic overcentralization is the failure to distinguish between equality before the law and the vicious perversion of equality that arises from the claim that all people have equal talents, equal mental and physical strength, and an equal desire to succeed. The wishful thinking that all individuals are born with equal abilities deepens the conflict between liberty and equal opportunities. Only totalitarian rulers offer a complete equality in mediocrity, which reduces all people down to the level of helplessness and impotence before the power of the government. Complete equality, by eliminating competition, eliminates also opportunities to all who can profitably use them.

The French Revolution of 1789 in its *Declaration of the Rights of Man and of Citizens* declared, "The law is an expression of the will of the community. . . . and all being equal in its sight, are equally eligible to all honours, places, and employments, according to their different abilities, without any other distinction than that created by their virtue and talents." The slogan calling for open competition to public appointments was "La carrière ouverte aux talents" (Careers open to talents).

President Lincoln, referring to the signers of the Declaration of Independence, commented:

"The authors of that notable instrument. . . . did not intend to declare all men equal in all respects. They did not mean to say that all men were equal in color, size, intellect, moral development, or social capacity. They defined with tolerable distinctness in what respect they consider all men created equal—'certain inalienable rights, among which are life, liberty, and the pursuit of happiness.' "

Happiness is not conferred upon mankind by the Creator, as life and liberty are. Man has the right to pursue happiness, and this right does not imply that all men and women are created equal in talent nor that they should be rewarded equally by society. People are not products of cloning, and equality should not be confused with uniformity. Under uniform standardization, outstanding achievements are frowned on and excellence is punished.

Equality in freedom means that (1) opportunities will be afforded to all persons in a free society where arbitrary or artificial barriers based on birth, economic status, race, religion, or sex do not exist; (2) in the open competition for scarce opportunities it is the responsibility of each person to apply himself or herself to the pursuit of such opportunities; and (3) the exceptional performance or industriousness, the extra efforts, and the special abilities that result in a high quality of goods or services should be rewarded.

Individual superiority, not uniform standardization; the use of people's abilities to the fullest limits of their capacity, not mediocrity; freedom to gain individual achievements by one's own efforts, not a subservience to egalitarianism—these will secure the progress and the prosperity that depend upon the continuous strengthening of excellence. A nation's long-term interest demands the rejection both of uniformity as the standard of performance and of the "egalitarian doctrine of justice." Our society has the responsibility to accept equal opportunity as an unquestionable right and to provide equal opportunity to all, based on capability, diligence, and performance. This passion for justice and equality is paralleled by the responsibility to push forward our intellectual forces to the highest level and to disregard the erroneous egalitarian doctrine of justice that calls for equality of results and rewards. By reconciling these two responsibilities, equality and freedom form an inseparable relationship.

The "New Egalitarians," who promulgate the doctrine of equality of results, expect the federal government to be "responsible not only for the total amount of national income, but for its distribution. . . ." (Christopher Jencks, *Inequality*, Basic Books, 1972, p. 264.) Equality, they argue, "cannot be defined solely in terms of opportunity, it must also be judged by results, by whether current inequalities of income and wealth, occupation, political power and the like are being reduced." (Herbert J. Gans, *More Equality*, Pantheon Books, 1973, p. xi.) In order to carry out the radically equal distribution of "all social primary goods," which also include "bases of social respect," such as social position, income, property, and rank, the "accidents of natural endowment" should be nullified. (John Rawls, *A Theory of Justice*, Belknap Press, Harvard, 1971, p. 15.)

The equality of results recommended by the New Egalitarians leans toward what Tocqueville called "the new despotism." He had this kind of equality in mind when he wrote that in order to succeed in centralizing the supreme power, the sole precondition required is to get people to believe that they love equality. According to Tocqueville, the single principle of the science of despotism is, "Every central power which follows its natural tendencies courts and encourages the principle of equality; for equality singularly facilitates, extends, and secures this influence of a central power." Egalitarian justice, by vesting in the government the responsibility for equal distribution of income and wealth, not only sacrifices economic expediency and the need for incentives but, what is more important, destroys our freedom, thus bringing into focus the central cause of the tension between liberty and equality.

Political Equality

People seek economic equality in the sense of enjoying a decent income, so as to provide the minimum needs of their families, such as decent shelter, decent educational opportunity, decent health care, and decent retirement benefits. They also seek political equality as well as civic and social equality. Political equality calls for an effective sharing of the political process that shapes the life of the community, of the state, and of the nation. It demands an opportunity for every citizen to participate in government on equal terms with everyone else. One of the landmark decisions in this field was the *Charles W. Baker v. Joe C. Carr* decision of March 26, 1962 (82 S. Ct. 691), which gave urban voters underrepresented in the state legislature a justiciable constitutional cause of action.

Until 1962 the courts had refused to intervene in controversies concerning the standards of fairness for a representative system. They had argued that it was beyond their competence to revise congressional representative districts in order to reflect the great changes that had taken place in the distribution of a state's population. The widely heralded case of *Colegrove v. Green* (66 S. Ct. 1198), which in the words of Justice Ramsey Clark had "served as Mother Hubbard to most of the subsequent cases" before *Baker v. Carr*, illustrates the now-abandoned position of the Supreme Court not to take action on issues of "a peculiarly political nature," such as legislative apportionment.

The following facts were essential to the *Colegrove v. Green* case. The Illinois legislature in 1901 established congressional election districts on the basis of the 1900 census. The state legislature was chosen on the basis of state election districts apportioned in a way similar to that of the 1901 congressional election districts. The federal census of 1910, of 1920, of 1930, and of 1940 each showed a great population shift among the districts established in 1901. But all attempts to have the state legislature reapportion congressional districts so as more nearly to equalize their population had been unsuccessful. Consequently, the congressional election districts had populations that ranged from 112,000 to 914,000. Three petitioners, citizens of Illinois, claimed that since they lived in the heavily populated districts, their vote was far less effective than that of people living in a much more sparsely populated district who also were allowed to choose one Congressman (some smaller districts were only one-ninth the population of some heavily populated districts). The petitioners contended that this reduction of the effectiveness of their vote resulted in legislative discrimination against them and thus amounted to a denial of the equal protection of the laws guaranteed by the Fourteenth Amendment.

The Supreme Court affirmed the dismissal of the complaint by the district court. Justice Felix Frankfurter, who announced the judgment, stated in his opinion that the Constitution precludes jurisdiction in this case since Article I, Section 4, has conferred upon Congress exclusive authority to secure fair representation by the states in the popular House and left to that House the determination of whether states have fulfilled their responsibility. (Article I, Section 4, provides that "the Times, Places and Manner of Holding Elections for. . . . Representatives, shall be prescribed in each State by the Legislature thereof; but the Congress may at any time by Law make or alter such Regulations. . . .") Consequently, the subject of whether Congress faithfully discharges its duty, argued Justice Frankfurter, has been committed to the exclusive control of Congress, and the judiciary has been "excluded by the clear intention of the Constitution." (Justices Stanley F. Reed and Harold H. Burton concurred with Justice Frankfurter's opinion.)

In a dissenting opinion, Justice Hugo Black pointed out that the Equal Protection Clause of the Fourteenth Amendment forbids discrimination that gives certain citizens a fractional vote and others a full vote. He agreed that such discrimination was taking place in Illinois. This discrimination, argued Justice Black, violated Article I of the Constitution, which provides that Congressmen "shall be. . . . chosen . . . by the People of the several States," and Section 2 of the Fourteenth Amendment, which provides that "Representatives shall be apportioned among the several States according to their respective numbers. . . ." In Justice Black's judgment, the courts, under the Constitution, have jurisdiction over geographical distribution of electoral strength among the state's political subdivisions. (Justice Black was joined in his dissent by Justices William O. Douglas and Frank Murphy; Justice John Rutledge, writing separately, expressed agreement with Justice Black's conclusion.)

The principle of equality before the law—which applies also to political equality—demanded the settlement of two controversial questions: First, should the Supreme Court intervene in matters of apportionment when the history of congressional apportionment "is its embroilment in politics, in the sense of party contests and party interest," and, second, is the right of every citizen to have an equally effective voice in electing his or her representatives— which is a right essential under a free government—a constitutional and federally protected right, and should the federal courts therefore provide a remedy to rectify any wrong done? The controversy aroused by these questions was settled by the U. S. Supreme Court in its decision of *Baker v. Carr* and in the one-person, one-vote decision of *Reynolds v. Sims* (377 U. S. 533 [1964].)

The facts in *Baker v. Carr* were similar to those in *Colegrove v. Green* (although in the latter case the appellants did not present an equal protection argument). In 1901 the Tennessee General Assembly, relying upon the federal census, passed an apportionment act. In the more than 60 years since that action, all reapportionment proposals in both Houses and the General Assembly had failed to pass in spite of the fact that, since 1901, Tennessee had experienced substantial growth and redistribution of population. The relative standings of the counties in terms of qualified voters also had changed substantially.

The complaint alleged that the 1901 statute had denied the appellants (plaintiffs in the district court) the equal protection of the laws accorded them by the Fourteenth Amendment to the Constitution "by virtue of the debasement of their votes." According to Justice Clark the apportionment in Tennessee was "a topsy-turvical of gigantic proportions . . . a crazy quilt without rational basis." The district court dismissed the case on two grounds: (1) that the court lacked jurisdiction over the subject matter and (2) that the complaint failed to state a claim upon which relief could be granted. The district court proceeded to explain that from a review of numerous Supreme Court decisions there could be no doubt that federal courts, "whether from lack of jurisdiction or from the inappropriateness of the subject matter for judicial consideration, will not intervene in cases of this type to compel legislative reapportionment."

The U. S. Supreme Court reversed the judgment of the district court, and the case was remanded for further proceedings consistent with the opinion delivered by Justice William Brennan. The Supreme Court held that a complaint containing allegations that a state statute effected an apportionment that deprived certain citizens of equal protection of the laws in violation of the Fourteenth Amendment presented an appropriate subject for judicial consideration.

Article III, Section 2, of the federal Constitution provides that "the judicial Power shall extend to all Cases, in Law and Equity, arising under this Constitution, the Laws of the United States, and Treaties made, or which shall be made, under their authority. . . ." The complaint alleged that the 1901 statute effected an apportionment that deprived the appellants of the equal protection of the law in violation of the Fourteenth Amendment, and, therefore, in the opinion of the Court there was a cause of action which "arises under" the federal Constitution. (Dismissal of the complaint upon the ground of lack of jurisdiction over the subject matter would be justified only if that claim were "so attenuated and unsubstantial as to be absolutely devoid of merit.")

The Court, by deciding that a citizen's right to vote is secured by the Constitution and that federal courts have jurisdiction over controversies concerning voting rights, did not imply that state legislatures must be so structured as to reflect with approximate equality the voice of every voter. There is no requirement that an apportionment plan must have mathematical exactness in its application. Only, as Justice Clark stated in a concurring opinion, where the total picture "reveals incommensurables of both magnitude and frequency can it be said that there is present an invidious discrimination."

The *Baker v. Carr* decision that apportionment cases present a justiciable controversy subject to adjudication by federal courts opened the door to challenges to existing apportionment plans under the Equal Protection Clause of the Fourteenth Amendment. The Supreme Court addressed the merits of six cases decided two years later, in 1964, announcing the "one-person, one-vote" requirement, which demanded that state legislative districts should be apportioned on the basis of population. The leading decision was issued in the case *B. A. Reynolds v. M. O. Sims*, involving legislative apportionment in Alabama. (377 U. S. 533 [1964].)

The plaintiffs in this case, residents and taxpayers of Jefferson County, noted that the last apportionment of the Alabama legislature was based on the 1900 federal census. They claimed that since population growth in the state from 1900 to 1960 had been uneven, numerous counties were victims of discrimination with respect to the allocation of legislative representation. Applying 1960 figures, only 25.9 percent of the state's total population resided in districts represented by a majority of the members of the Senate. Population variance ratios of up to about 41-to-1 existed in the Senate and up to about 16-to-1 in the House. Thus Jefferson County, with more than 600,000 people, was given only one senator, as were Lowndes County, with a 1960 population of only 15,417, and Wilcox County, with only 18,739. With respect to the allocation of seats in the Alabama House, Mobile County, with a population of 314,301, was given three seats and Jefferson County, with 634,864 people, had seven, whereas Bullock County, with a population of only 13,426, and Henry County, with only 15,286, were allocated two seats each.

On July 12, 1962, the Alabama legislature adopted two reapportionment plans to take effect for the 1966 elections. One, referred to as the "67-Senator Amendment," provided for a House of Representatives consisting of 106 members, apportioned by giving one seat to each of Alabama's 67 counties and distributing the others according to population by the "equal proportions" method. The Senate was to be composed of 67 members, one from each county.

The other reapportionment plan, referred to as the Crawford-Webb Act, provided for a Senate consisting of 35 members, representing 35 senatorial districts established along county lines. In apportioning the 106 seats in the Alabama House of Representatives, the act gave each county one seat and apportioned the remaining 39 on a population basis.

On July 21, 1962, the district court considered both the 67-Senator Amendment and the Crawford-Webb Act and concluded that they were totally unacceptable since neither of them met the necessary constitutional requirements. The court found that each of the legislative acts was discriminatory, arbitrary, and irrational. In reference to the so-called federal analogy of senatorial apportionment based on a geographical basis, the court found it irrelevant because of the dramatically opposing history of the requirements of the federal Constitution and the Alabama Constitution.

On July 25, 1962, the court—directing its concern

to finding a remedy—ordered into effect for the November 1962 election a provisional and temporary reapportionment phase composed of the 67-Senator Amendment provisions relating to the House of Representatives and the Crawford-Webb Act provisions relating to the Senate. The court emphasized that its action would not suffice as a permanent reapportionment. The court also enjoined state officials from holding future elections under any of the apportionment plans that it had found invalid.

The plaintiffs and the defendants appealed the decision of the district court to the Supreme Court of the United States. On June 15, 1964, the Supreme Court held that the existing apportionment and the two proposed legislative plans for reapportionment of the seats in the two houses of the Alabama legislature were invalid under the Equal Protection Clause in that the apportionment was not based on population and was completely lacking in rationality. The Court affirmed the judgment of the district court and remanded the cases for further proceedings consistent with the views stated in the opinion.

The Court's opinion stressed the undeniable, constitutionally protected right of all qualified citizens to vote, in state as well as in federal elections. The right of suffrage is a fundamental matter in a free and democratic society. Legislators, stated the Court, "represent people, not trees or acres. . . . Legislators are elected by voters, not farms or economic interests." Considerations of area alone provide, therefore, "an insufficient justification for deviations from the equal-population principle." This principle is fundamental for a representative government.

Equal representation for equal numbers of people and the right to vote freely for candidates of one's choice are the essence of a democratic society. The district court did not err, stated the Supreme Court, in holding that neither of the two proposed plans to remedy the existing crazy-quilt apportionment in Alabama met the necessary constitutional requirements. The Supreme Court agreed with the district court that no conceivable analogy could be drawn between the federal scheme of allocating two Senate seats in the federal Congress to each of the 50 states, regardless of population, and the apportionment of seats in the Alabama legislature under the proposed 67-Senator Amendment.

The system of representation in the two Houses of the federal Congress was one conceived out of compromise and concessions in order to avert a deadlock in the Constitutional Convention that had threatened to abort the birth of our nation. In establishing federalism, the formerly independent states bound themselves under one national government. It was not their intention to establish a pattern for the apportionment of seats in state legislatures. Counties, cities, or other political subdivisions serve as subordinates to the state governmental instrumentalities created by a state to assist in carrying out governmental functions. They were never considered as independently sovereign entities. Therefore, stated the Court, the 67-Senator Amendment for apportioning seats in the Alabama legislature could not be sustained by recourse to the so-called federal analogy and did not meet the requirements of the Equal

Protection Clause. The Supreme Court concluded, however, that the action taken by the district court, ordering into effect a reapportionment of both houses of the Alabama Legislature for purposes of the 1962 primary elections by using the best parts of the two proposed plans (which the Court found, as a whole, to be invalid), was "an appropriate and well considered exercise of judicial power."

The plan ordered by the district court was intended only as a temporary and provisional measure, not to be sustained as the basis for conducting the 1966 election of the Alabama legislature. Further evidence of an appropriate exercise of judicial power, stated the Supreme Court, is the intent of the district court to take some additional action should the reapportioned Alabama legislature "fail to enact a constitutionally valid, permanent apportionment scheme in the interim. . . ."

As Justice Clark, who concurred in the Supreme Court decision, pointed out, the "equal population" principle for state legislative apportionment discussed above is an "offshoot" of the one-person, one-vote principle that the Supreme Court stated in *Gray v. Sanders*: "The conception of political equality from the Declaration of Independence, to Lincoln's Gettysburg Address, to the Fifteenth, Seventeenth, and Nineteenth Amendments can mean only one thing—one person, one vote." (372 U. S. 368, 381 [1963].)

The *Wesberry v. Sanders* decision, built upon *Gray v. Sanders*, stated that congressional representation must be based on population "as nearly as is practicable." (376 U. S. 1, 8 [1964].) Without diluting the equal-population principle, more flexibility may be constitutionally permissible in legislative apportionment than in congressional districting because of the significantly larger number of seats in the state legislative bodies to be distributed within a state.

In numerous other decisions the Supreme Court ascertained that there are no cognizable principles that would justify a departure from the basic standard of equality among voters in the apportionment of seats in state legislatures. Diluting the weight of votes because of place of residence, economic status, or race impairs basic constitutional rights under the Fourteenth Amendment and strikes at the heart of representative government. The Equal Protection Clause demands substantially equal state legislative representation for all citizens in all places and of all races.

This right of voters to judicial protection under the Equal Protection Clause remade the political map of the United States and brought a political balance between urban and rural areas. (At the time of the one-person, one-vote decisions, rural areas held, nationwide, nearly twice as many legislative seats as they would have been entitled to by an apportionment based on the equal-population principle.)

It should be mentioned that before the case of *Baker v. Carr* reversed a uniform course of decision established by numerous earlier cases, the Supreme Court applied the Fifteenth Amendment to strike down a redrafting of municipal boundaries which effected a discriminatory impairment of voting rights. In the case of *Gomillion v. Lightfoot*, the plaintiff, Gomillion—a Negro who had been a resident of

Tuskogee, Alabama, until the municipal boundaries were so recast by the state legislature as to exclude practically all Negroes—claimed deprivation of the right to vote in municipal elections. (364 U. S. 339 [1960].)

The Supreme Court unanimously reversed the decision of the district court, which had been affirmed by the court of appeals for want of jurisdiction and a failure to state a claim upon which relief could be granted. In response to the argument (endorsed by *Colegrove v. Green*) that states enjoyed unrestricted control over municipal boundaries, the Court responded that Gomillion was lifted "out of the so-called 'political' arena and into the conventional sphere of constitutional litigation" because there was discriminatory treatment of a racial minority, which violated the Fifteenth Amendment. State power exercised within the domain of state interest may be insulated from federal judicial review, but, stated the Court, "such insulation is not carried over when state power is used as an instrument for circumventing a federally protected right." (*Gomillion v. Lightfoot, Ibid.*, p. 347.)

The right to vote is inherent in the republican form of government envisaged by Article IV, Section 4, of the Constitution. The Fifteenth and Nineteenth Amendments provide barriers to a state's freedom in prescribing qualifications of voters. Race, color, religion, and sex are impermissible standards that would permit a state to weight the vote of one county or one district more heavily than another. The Equal Protection Clause does not permit a state legislature to discriminate against the "underrepresented" counties or districts in favor of the "overrepresented" counties or districts in the collection and distribution of various taxes, tax revenues, and school and highway improvement funds. Legislators have no immunity from the Constitution; they are, stated the Court, "as responsive to the Constitution of the United States as are the citizens who elect [them]."

The fact that federal courts have jurisdiction over controversies concerning voting rights does not turn them into forums for political debate. The "right to have one's vote counted" is not a "political question" but one of civil rights, which include the right to vote, a right that lends itself to judicial standards and judicial remedies. The chief function of the courts, as John Rutledge (later Chief Justice) stated about 200 years ago in the course of the Constitutional Convention, is to secure the national rights. The right to vote, indispensable for the representative form of government, is one of these national rights and fundamental principles upon which our government is based.

Civil, Legal, and Social Equality

Among the types of equality that people seek and achieve by overthrowing the barriers of race and sex and in which our society seems greatly interested are civil, or legal, and social equalities. The right to serve on juries or the right to belong to associations of a person's own choosing are examples of such equalities. The courts and civil rights legislation press for constitutional prohibitions of discriminational practices and for the removal of conditions under which people cannot enjoy equal power in participation in group life.

As early as in 1880 the Supreme Court struck down a state statute that denied to Negroes on account of race participation as jurors in the administration of justice. Such a statute was held to contravene the main purpose of the Fourteenth Amendment. The very fact, wrote the Court,

> "that colored people are singled out and expressly denied by a statute all right to participate in the administration of the law, as jurors, because of their color, though they are citizens, and may be in other respects fully qualified, is practically a brand upon them, affixed by the law, an assertion of their inferiority, and a stimulant to that race prejudice which is an impediment to securing to individuals of the race that equal justice which the law aims to secure to all others." (*Strauder v. State of Virginia*, 100 U. S. 308 [1880].)

This set of principles was explicitly reaffirmed and repeatedly applied in many cases coming before the Court. These well-established principles include the prima facie proof of systematic discrimination when citizens because of race are excluded from jury service for an extended period of time. This "rule of exclusion" became an indisputable fact in a case, for instance, when no black had served on a jury for a period of 30 years. When such a situation occurred, stated the Court, "it became the duty of the State to try to justify such an exclusion as having been brought about for some reason other than racial discrimination." (*Patton v. State of Mississippi*, 332 U. S. 466 [1947]; see also the case of *Hernandez v. State of Texas*, 347 U. S. 480 [1954].)

Racial discrimination that results in the exclusion from jury service of otherwise qualified groups because of their race not only violates our Constitution but, as the Court stated, "is at war with our basic concepts of a democratic society and a representative government." (*Smith v. State of Texas*, 311 U. S. 128, 130 [1940].)

Also at war with our basic concepts of democracy are discriminatory practices conflicting with social equality—practices that deny any person full access to publicly available goods and services. Since social equality demands such access, the question arose whether this access should extend to private organizations' membership practices. Some have sought to find shelter for these practices, which quite often have been discriminatory, under the umbrella of the First Amendment.

It is beyond debate that freedom of association is an indispensable means of preserving other individual liberties assured by the First Amendment, which embraces freedom of speech, assembly, petition for redress of grievances, and the exercise of religion. Although the word "association" is not listed among the constitutionally protected rights, the Supreme Court has repeatedly acknowledged freedom of association as one of the rights derived by implication from the written First Amendment guarantees.

Finding an answer to the question of whether the commitment to social equality applies also to membership practices of private organizations required the courts to address the conflict between a state's effort to eliminate discrimination on the basis of gender, race, nationality, origin, or religion against its citizens seeking membership in private organizations and the constitutional freedom of association asserted by members of these private organizations.

In one line of decisions, the Supreme Court has concluded that certain intimate human relationships must be secured against intrusion by the state because of the role of such relationships in safeguarding the individual freedoms that are essential to our form of government. Interference by the state with individuals' selection of whom they wish to join in a common endeavor for the advancement of beliefs and ideas or with whom they have strong personal bonds may violate the guaranteed freedom of association.

In another set of decisions, the Court has recognized a right to associate with others in pursuit of a wide variety of political, social, economic, educational, religious, and cultural needs. This right reflects the commitment to eliminating discrimination because of race, color, creed, religion, national origin, or sex and to assuring its citizens equal access and enjoyment of publicly available goods, services, and facilities.

The right to social equality is not absolute, since it comes in contact with boundaries of the right to associate with others. Within the broad range of human relationships, there are certain zones of privacy, such as marriage, procreation, contraception, cohabitation with relatives, or child rearing and education, that are protected from government interference. On the other hand, there are innumerable commercial associations that enjoy a minimal constitutional protection since their activities are not predominantly of the type protected by the First Amendment. For instance, according to the U. S. Supreme Court, chapters of the United States Jaycees and of Rotary International lack the distinctive characteristics that may afford constitutional protection to the decision of their members to exclude women.

The United States Jaycees is a nonprofit national membership corporation whose objective is to pursue such educational and charitable purposes as will promote and foster the growth and development of young men's civic organizations. Regular membership is limited to young men between ages 18 and 35, whereas women may purchase only associate membership. An associate member may not vote, hold local or national office, or receive achievement awards. In 1974, the Minneapolis and St. Paul, Minnesota, local chapters had, in defiance of the bylaws, admitted women as regular members and, as a result, had had a number of sanctions imposed by the national organization of the Jaycees. When those two local chapters were informed that revocation of their charters was to be considered, members of both chapters filed discrimination charges with the Minnesota Department of Human Rights, challenging the Jaycees' policy of forbidding women the same membership status as men.

The Minnesota Human Rights Act forbids discrimination on the basis of sex in "places of public accommodation." The United States District Court upheld the application of the act to the Jaycees. The Court of Appeals for the Eighth Circuit reversed the decision, holding that the application of the act to the Jaycees would produce a "direct and substantial" interference with the Jaycees' freedom of association guaranteed by the First Amendment and that the act was vague as construed and applied and hence unconstitutional under the Due Process Clause of the Fourteenth Amendment.

The U. S. Supreme Court reversed the judgment of the court of appeals by taking the position that the individual's rights provided by the First Amendment could not be protected from interference by the state "unless a correlative freedom to engage in group effort toward those ends were not also guaranteed." Therefore, the Court stated, because of the compelling interest in eradicating discrimination against women, the application of the Minnesota act to the Jaycees forcing it to accept women as regular members does not abridge either the male members' freedom of intimate association or their freedom of expressive association. The Court also did not find the Minnesota Human Rights Act unconstitutionally vague, because it articulates its aims with a reasonable degree of clarity. (*Kathryn R. Roberts v. United States Jaycees*, 468 U. S. 609 [1984].)

The Supreme Court took a similar position in the case of *Board of Directors of Rotary International v. Rotary Club of Duarte*. (107 S. Ct. 1940 [1987].) Rotary International is a nonprofit corporation composed of local Rotary Clubs. It is an "organization of business and professional men united worldwide who provide humanitarian service, encourage high ethical standards in all vocations, and help build goodwill and peace in the world." Membership in Rotary Clubs is open only to men. Although women are permitted to attend meetings, give speeches, receive awards, and form auxiliary organizations, the Rotary constitution excludes women from membership.

In 1977 the Rotary Club of Duarte, California, admitted three women to active membership, and the board of directors of Rotary International revoked its charter and terminated its membership in Rotary International. The Duarte Club and two of its women members filed a complaint in the California Superior Court for the County of Los Angeles. The court found that Rotary Clubs do not provide their members with goods, services, or facilities and that business benefits are only incidental to the principal purposes of the association. Consequently, the court entered judgment for Rotary International.

The California Court of Appeals reversed this judgment. It held that the California Superior Court had erred in finding that the business advantages afforded by membership in a local Rotary Club are merely incidental. The court of appeals also rejected the trial court's finding that the Duarte Club does not provide goods, services, or facilities to its members. Rotary Clubs, rather than carrying on their activities in an atmosphere of privacy, seek to keep their "windows and doors open to the world." By opening membership to leading business and professional women, stated the Supreme Court when it reviewed the case, Rotary Clubs "are likely to obtain a more representative cross-section of community leaders with a broadened capacity for service." As in the *Roberts* case, the U. S. Supreme Court stressed that the state's compelling interest in assuring equal access to women extends to the acquisition of leadership skills and business contacts as well as tangible goods and services. The judgment of the Court of Appeals of California was affirmed.

In the light of the two U. S. Supreme Court decisions described above, the definition of goods, services, and public accommodations reaches various forms of public and quasi-commercial conduct. This expansive definition, stated the Court in the *Roberts* case, "reflects a recognition of the changing nature of the American economy and of the importance, both to the individual and to society, of removing both barriers to economic advancement and political and social integration that have historically plagued certain disadvantaged groups, including women."

Equality Among Nations

The recognition of the importance of "removing the barriers" to the advancement of equality goes beyond national boundaries. Human dignity—the essential working principle of equality—when applied to international relations means faith in the dignity of each nation, poor or opulent, militarily powerful or weak. It means progress in the direction of a free family of nations safeguarded by the rule of law and the principle of equality before the law.

Equality among nations was advocated by the French mathematician and philosopher Marie Jean Antoine Nicolas Caritat, Marquis de Condorcet, who took part in the French Revolution. He traced human development through nine epochs to the outbreak of the revolution and predicted the abolition of inequalities in the tenth epoch, which would follow the revolution. He argued that the rights of women should be equal with the rights of men and that freedom demanded the equality of rights among nations. (For opposing the cruelty of the Jacobins, Condorcet was put in prison, where he died.)

After World War I, the aim of peace through the equality of all nations was outlined by President Woodrow Wilson as follows: "No special or separate interest of any single nation or any group of nations can be made the basis of any part of the settlement which is not consistent with the common interest of all." (The "Five Particulars" of September 27, 1918.) "Every territorial settlement . . . must be made in the interest of and for the benefit of the populations concerned, and not as a part of any mere adjustment or compromise of claims among rival States." (The "Four Principles" of February 11, 1918.) After World War II, the peoples of Bulgaria, Czechoslovakia, Hungary, Poland, Rumania, and other "captive" nations could wonder whether their "equality" and destinies were not sacrificed on the altar of "compromise of claims among rival states" with disregard to the "benefit of the populations concerned."

Following World War II, human rights demanding economic and political equality were recognized by the Universal Declaration of Human Rights, approved by the United Nations General Assembly in 1948. The first group of human rights listed includes the right to the economic necessities of life and to fulfillment of such vital needs as food, shelter, health care, and education. The second group includes the opportunity to participate in one's government and the right to enjoy the civil and political liberties, such as freedom of thought, of assembly, of the press, of speech, of religion, and of moving freely both within and outside one's own country. These demands remained only words, proclaimed with no intention of enforcement.

The Charter of the United Nations provides that the General Assembly will assist "in the realization of human rights and fundamental freedoms for all without distinction as to race, sex, language, or religion. . . ." (Article 13.) The demands enshrined in the universal declaration enunciated by the General Assembly include the right to social security; to periodic holidays with pay; to security in the event of unemployment, sickness, disability, widowhood, old age, or lack of livelihood in circumstances beyond a person's control; and to an education that shall be free in the "elementary and fundamental stages" and other rights which in numerous countries have never become a fact and have remained an unobtainable ideal, with no expectation of any assistance from the General Assembly.

Strides in the Direction of Equality

To make equality work it is imperative to understand what equality is. The Declaration of Independence and the Constitution place great emphasis on liberty but take equality among individuals for granted, simply declaring that "all men are created equal." These historical documents do not refer to an equal distribution of income or to the removal of disparities of wealth. Equality of opportunity or equality before the law means the right to open competition and to a similarity of treatment under the rule of law, with all being equal in its sight.

Even such great historical documents—which are triumphs for the highest aspirations of mankind—remain mere words unless there is an understanding of their meaning and a willingness to act to implement them. In this country we have made great strides in the direction of equality, to mention only the progressive income tax; the public school system; the drive for equal voting privileges regardless of gender, race, or color; and such measures as Social Security, Medicare, the guaranteed minimum wage, old-age pensions, and recent civil rights legislation. There will always be a gap between what we want and what we can accomplish. There will always be a time for grander goals that seem to elude our grasp. The goals we have been seeking for so long, however, will never be achieved by confusing equality with an egalitarianism that decries excellence in achievement and that detracts from our national purpose. When its focus shifts from equality of opportunity to equality in the distribution of goods and services, the spirit of equality is destroyed.

Referring to the spirit of liberty, President Lincoln once said, "Our defense is in the spirit which prized liberty as the heritage of all men, in all lands, everywhere. Destroy this spirit and you have the seeds of despotism at your own front." Paraphrasing this warning we can say, "Destroy the spirit of equality by trying to assure for all equal income, equal wealth, equal position, equal power for mental development, and equal influence and you can expect to have 'the seeds of despotism at your own front.' "

CHAPTER 2

TOLERANCE

Conflicting Views

In 1977 the American Nazi Party requested permission to hold a demonstration in Skokie, Illinois. The Circuit Court of Cook County, Illinois, issued an injunction barring the Nazis from "marching, walking or parading or otherwise displaying the swastika on or off their persons; [or] distributing pamphlets or displaying any materials which incite or promote hatred against persons of Jewish faith or ancestry or hatred against persons of any faith or ancestry, race or religion."

The Illinois Appellate Court held that the injunction was a restraint of activity protected by the First Amendment. The Court allowed the Nazis to demonstrate but did not allow the Nazis to display the swastika, since "the tens of thousands of Skokie Jewish residents must feel gross revulsion for the swastika and would immediately respond to the personally abusive epithets slung their way in the form of the defendant's chosen symbol, the swastika." (*Village of Skokie v. National Socialist Party of America*, 366 N.E. 2d 347 [1977].)

On January 27, 1978, the Illinois Supreme Court ruled that neither the swastika emblem nor the march could be prohibited. The court took the position that the swastika represents a symbolic act of speech that conveys the beliefs of those who wear it.

Therefore, the display of the swastika, as offensive as it may be, stated the court, cannot be precluded for the reason that it may "provoke a violent reaction by those who view it. Particularly this is true where, as here, there has been advance notice by the demonstrators of their plans . . . . A speaker who gives prior notice of his message has not compelled a confrontation with those who voluntarily listen." The injunction was vacated. The three new ordinances adopted by Skokie which were intended to control demonstrations were nullified as unconstitutional by the decision of the Federal Court for the Northern District of Illinois, affirmed by the Seventh Circuit Court of Appeals. (*Collin v. Smith*, 578 F.2d 1197, 7th Cir. [1978].)

No democracy can survive without freedom of speech, which is the essence of tolerance. This freedom, protected by the Constitution, is, however, not absolute at all times and under all circumstances; the lack of uniformity in the U.S. Supreme Court's interpretation of the law pertaining to inflammatory speeches or action such as we have been discussing, known as the "fighting words doctrine," is evidence of this lack. Thus the U.S. Supreme Court has affirmed the constitutionality of statutes that prohibit obscenity or defamation and has affirmed the state's power to punish an utterance directed at a defined group, unless it is "a willful and purposeless restriction unrelated to the peace and well being of the State." (*Beauharnais v. Illinois*, 343 U.S. 250, 258, 72 S.Ct. 725, 731 [1952].)

In this case, Joseph Beauharnais, president of a fascist organization known as the White Circle League, was convicted for distributing in public places, in violation of the Illinois Criminal Code, leaflets portraying "depravity, criminality, unchastity or lack of virtue of citizens of Negro race and color." The Court in confirming the Illinois statutes referred to the tragic experience of the states that have been the scene of exacerbated tension between races, often flaring into violence and destruction. The Illinois legislature did have good reason, stated the Court, to seek ways to curb malicious defamation of racial and religious groups, made in public places and by means calculated to incite violence and breaches of the peace.

Such transgressions the states may punish appropriately. The Court found unconvincing the argument that the choice the Supreme Court opened to legislatures may be abused and can be only a step away from prohibiting libel of a political party. Every power may be abused, and the possibility of abuse is a poor reason for denying the state legislature the right to adopt measures against criminal libels "sanctioned by centuries of Anglo-American law."

The same position was taken by the U.S. Supreme Court in the case of *Chaplinsky v. New Hampshire*. Chaplinsky, a member of the sect known as Jehovah's Witnesses, while proselytizing on the streets of Rochester, New Hampshire, denounced all religions as a "racket." When arrested for disturbing the peace, he insulted the city marshal by calling him "a damned fascist" and a "goddamned racketeer." The Court, following the "fighting words" doctrine, found that Chaplinsky's utterances were not "an essential part of any exposition of ideas" and were "of such slight social value as a step to truth that any benefit that may be derived from them is clearly outweighed by the social interests in order and morality." The Court unanimously affirmed a conviction based on a statute of the state of New Hampshire that banned speeches that could inflict injury or an immediate breach of the peace. (315 U.S. 568, 572, 62 S.Ct. 766, 769 [1942].)

An analysis of the meaning of violence we find in the position adopted by the Supreme Court that advocacy of violence merely used as a means of accomplishing political reform is constitutionally protected and should be distinguished from advocacy of violence intended to incite imminent unlawful conduct. (*Brandenburg v. Ohio*, 395 U.S. 444, 446, 89 S.Ct. 1827, 1829 [1969].) In this case, Brandenburg, a leader of the Ku Klux Klan convicted under an Ohio Criminal Syndicalism statute, stated: "We are not a revengent organization, but if our President, our Congress, our Supreme Court, continues to suppress the white caucasian race, it's possible that there might have to be some revengeance taken." The Court reversed the conviction because the constitutionality of the Criminal Syndicalism Act could not be sustained; it makes no distinction between mere advocacy of violence from preparing a group for violent action and steeling it to such action.

The United States Supreme Court took a similar position in the *Terminiello v. City of Chicago* case. The Court overturned a "breach of the peace" conviction based on an ordinance of the city of Chicago, which as construed by the trial court included in "breach of the peace" any speech which "stirs the public to anger, incites dispute, brings about a condition of unrest, or creates a disturbance. . . ." In this case, a suspended Catholic priest named Terminiello, in an address delivered in an auditorium in Chicago under the auspices of the Christian Veterans of America, criticized various racial and political groups whose activities he denounced as inimical to the nation's welfare. At the meeting, he hurled at the inflamed mob of his adversaries such epithets as "slimy scum," "snakes," "bedbugs," and the like. Disturbances caused by a turbulent and angry crowd ensued. The convictions for "breach of the peace" were affirmed by both the Illinois Appellate and the Illinois Supreme Courts.

The United States Supreme Court reversed the conviction because parts of the Chicago ordinance were unconstitutional. The function of free speech, stated the Court, "is to invite dispute. It may indeed best serve its high purpose when it induces a condition of unrest, creates dissatisfaction with conditions as they are, or even stirs people in anger. . . . That is why freedom of speech, though not absolute, . . . is nevertheless protected against censorship orpunishment, unless shown likely to produce a *clear and present danger of a serious substantive evil that rises far above public inconvenience, annoyance, or unrest.*" (337 U.S. 1, 4, 69 S.Ct. 894, 896 [1949]. Emphasis added.)

The apparent contradictions in the decisions of the Courts which we have been discussing raise a number of questions: Is there a constitutional obligation to tolerate groups or individuals who advocate violence or who deride or discredit a class of citizens of a certain creed, religion, race, or color? What kind of unrest and disturbance must violence create in order to rise "far above public inconvenience, annoyance, or unrest" and to justify the employment of the "clear and present danger" provision of the violence test? Are not outbreaks of violence, lynching, or rioting as a rule incited by hatred and passion supplied by speeches to some mass of people? What restraint should be placed on the extent of tolerance of actions that advocate a resort to force and violence so as to preserve a balance between tolerance and other values which are essential for democracies to function properly, including freedom of speech, freedom of the press, freedom of worship, and other fundamental personal rights and liberties? Are there rules and procedures democracies should pursue to keep violent tendencies in check? Where is the real defense line?

A Definition of Tolerance

In order to answer these questions, it will be helpful to define the concept of tolerance and to outline a brief history of its development. Tolerance derives from the Latin *tolerantia*, a term intended to give the notion of bearing without repugnance, of enduring or putting up with. The term "tolerance" presupposes opposition or objection to a certain idea, behavior, or thing, and its ultimate acceptance. It reflects a self-restraint that permits us to reconcile our disapproval of certain opinions and practices with our acceptance of the right of others to pursue them. Such acceptance is not a sign of weakness. It suggests an attitude of putting up with people, **not of giving in to them.**

This self-restraint represents a concession and not always an absence of prejudice. A prejudiced person can be tolerant when he checks his impulses, blocks any action based upon his objection, and accepts the things toward which he is prejudiced. A businessman may be prejudiced against a certain minority group but be tolerant in his employment policies by constraining his prejudice and by not permitting himself to translate his negative attitude into discrimination.

Tolerance should not be confused with indifference. While tolerance reflects genuine disagreement, indifference marks absence of compulsion, interest, or concern about something. Lack of concern, for instance, whether a group claiming to be a religious sect or its leaders are engaged in fraudulent activities or are worshipping according to the beliefs of its members, is not tolerance but a socially harmful attitude. Such an attitude reflects neither a real objection to nor a real acceptance of the right to exist— the two prerequisites of tolerance.

Intolerance

Tolerance of intolerance aggravates intolerance. There are those who invoke tolerance as part of a strategy of overthrowing democracy, with which tolerance is closely associated as one of its fundamental principles. In our times, an appeal for tolerance has been used by fascists and communists in their efforts to destroy democracy. Goebbels stated: "When democracy granted democratic methods for us in times of opposition, this [Nazi seizure of power] was bound to happen in a democratic system. However, we National Socialists never asserted that we represented a democratic point of view, but we have declared openly that we used democratic methods only in order to gain the power and that, after assuming the power, we would deny to our adversaries without any consideration the means which were granted to us in times of (our) opposition." (*1 Nazi Conspiracy & Aggression* [GPO 1946] 202, Docs. 2500-PS, 2412-PS.)

Similarly, the communists continue to claim that their right to convey their political ideas in our country is protected by the First Amendment, and consequently they have the right to give speeches, engage in demonstrations, and advocate in their publications the overthrow of our duly elected government by force. History shows that, once they succeed in destroying an organized free society, the dictatorship they offer means, according to Lenin, "nothing more nor less than completely unrestricted power, absolutely unimpeded by laws or regulations and resting directly on the use of force." With the destruction of a free society, they destroy all civil liberties and the security of freedom enjoyed in a democratic State. The diabolical outrages against human personality thus perpetrated are motivated by the fact that the "solidarity and the internal unity of the Party" cannot afford "to be too liberal or permit freedom of factions." (Joseph Stalin, *Problems of Leninism*, Foreign Language Publishing House, Moscow, 1952, p. 175.)

In maintaining a democratic policy of political tolerance we must recognize that intolerance of intolerance safeguards tolerance. The foundation of a democratic system is endangered if there is no protection against the excesses of unrestrained abuses committed by those who advocate the adoption of communism or another form of totalitarian regime. They use or enhance mob violence, race rioting, and all kinds of public disorders in order to suppress—once they come to power—our liberties. The choice is not between tolerance and order. It is between tolerance with order and anarchy without order. Adherence to the doctrinaire logic that civil liberty means removal of all restraints may convert the constitutional guarantees on which our democracy is based into a suicide pact.

History demonstrates that tolerance of intolerance is suicidal for civil liberties and human rights. We can hardly be reminded too often that there was a Socrates who devoted himself to the intellectual and moral improvement of the Athenians by spending his life talking wherever men congregated about justice, knowledge, piety, and other moral values. When Athens was ruined by the Peloponnesian War, Socrates was sacrificed by the bigotry of the city, which made him responsible for the collapse of the Athenian virtues. When brought to trial, he was convicted for impiety, immorality, and corruption of youth and was condemned to drink the poison hemlock. Socrates, one of the most eminent thinkers in the history of mankind, was put to death as a criminal.

Religious Intolerance

Reinhold Niebuhr wrote that "the worst form of

intolerance is religious intolerance, in which the particular interests of the contestants hide behind religious absolutes." (*The Nature and Destiny of Man*, Vol. I, Charles Scribner's Sons, 1941, pp. 200–210.)

The history of the organized church teems with instances of intolerance and persecution of religious movements against the authority and the worldly interests of the church. Religious toleration was condemned as a heresy. Religious intolerance asserted itself externally in crusades or holy wars and internally in persecution. In one holy war, for instance, Charlemagne gave the Saxons and the Bohemians the choice between baptism and death. With fire and sword he carried the Gospel of the Cross down to the Adriatic coast and drove the Moslems back from the Pyrenees as far as Barcelona.

As for those who dissented within the church, "heretics" were executed—burned to death and hanged. Catholics as well as early Protestants persecuted dissident sects mercilessly. The twelfth-century monk Arnold de Brescia, who advocated the idea that possession of property was an exclusive right of lay powers and that the church had no right to hold property, was tried and executed by the Roman Curia. The Italian Dominican friar Savonarola (1452–1498), who preached against the corruption of society and predicted the forthcoming punishment of the church and its regeneration, was hanged by the Florentine government after it had forced him to confess that he was not a prophet.

John Wycliff, whose translation of the Bible was an important landmark in the history of English literature, was condemned twice as a heretic for spreading the doctrine that the Scriptures are the supreme authority. He was the forerunner of the Reformation, and in 1419 the Pope ordered the burning of his books. Huss, the Bohemian religious reformer and the leading opponent of the condemnation of Wycliff's writings, at the invitation of Emperor Sigismund and under the protection of the emperor's safe-conduct, presented himself at the Council of Constance, only to be imprisoned, tried, and burned at the stake as a heretic.

In 1616 the Copernican theory of the solar system was denounced by the Church as dangerous to faith. When Galileo, the great Italian astronomer and physicist, in his *Dialogue of the Two Chief Systems of the World* of 1632 confirmed the acceptance of the Copernican theory, he was tried by the Inquisition and obliged to abjure the "error" in his belief that the sun is the central body and the earth with the other planets revolves around it. His indefinite imprisonment was ended only by Pope Urban VIII.

Just as the Catholics used execution as a means to wipe out "heresy," so the early Protestants thought that any opposition to their religious practices implied evil that had to be eradicated. Michael Servetus, the Spanish physician and theologian (1511–1553), was condemned by Calvin for his antitrinitarian writings. By Calvin's order he was seized in Geneva, and after a long trial was burned at the stake on October 27, 1553. Like the Catholics, the early Protestants believed that if a man remained outside their faith he was condemned to burn forever in hell, and therefore he should be compelled even by torture to change his beliefs by force. Such conversion was deemed to save his soul and provide him with eternal life.

The leaders of the church in the Middle Ages, advocating persecution for religious nonconformity, argued that they were acting in accordance with Christ's commandment, "Go out on the highways and hedgerows and make them come in." (Luke 14:23.) The literal interpretation of this commandment (*compelle intrare*—"make them come in") was attributed to St. Augustine; it justified intolerance and forced conversion. When torture was used as a means of conversion, the leaders of the church maintained, the pain caused by forced coercion was nothing to what heretics and schismatics would suffer in hell, where men who remain outside the faith are condemned to burn forever. If a man died in the process of torture, at least he was rewarded with eternal life.

Religious Toleration

In the sixteenth and seventeenth centuries, a concern for religious toleration arose, and in the nineteenth and twentieth centuries, a similar concern for political tolerance grew up. (We use both the terms "toleration" and "tolerance." "Toleration" is identified with religion, while the term "tolerance" applies to political controversies. The modern concept of tolerance has its origin in religious "toleration," but both types of tolerance—or toleration—reflect opposition to intolerance.) Starting with the sixteenth century, numerous writers saw in ecclesiastical power and forcible conversion the root of intolerance and came to realize that in a healthy society men have to tolerate one another's political, religious, and philosophical differences. We shall briefly review the ideas of two brilliant representatives of this Age of Enlightenment, of this age of Reason and Knowledge—F.M.A. de Voltaire and John Locke. Both of them were greatly influenced by French philosopher Pierre Bayle (1647–1706), the Huguenot author of the *Traité de la tolerance universelle*, published in 1686.

Bayle believed that each person has the untrammeled and unquestionable right to worship God according to the dictates of his own conscience. Persecution or attempts to coerce a person to worship God in a particular way, stated Bayle, will never result in conviction, but will only produce hypocrites or martyrs. (He tolerated the atheist but denied, however, the right of religious liberty to the Catholic church, which should not in his judgment be tolerated because it actively and persistently promoted intolerance.) Forced conversion, according to Bayle, could not be reconciled with Christ's commandments of love for our fellowman, charity, forgiveness, and respect for human dignity. It is a sacrilegious offense to God Himself.

The tolerance advocated by Bayle was based on the principle of doubt concerning the substance of truth. To him it appeared impossible to define or to know with certainty "que la Verité que nous paroit est la Verité absolue"—that the truth that appears to us is the absolute truth. Bayle's position reminds us that when Jesus was asked by Pontius Pilate whether He was a king, He replied, "My task is to bear witness to the truth. For this was I born; for this I came into the world, and all who are not deaf to truth listen to my voice." Scholars have not yet agreed to a definition of what this truth is.

Because of this uncertainty and the commitment to search for the substance of truth, Bayle believed that "la Religion est une affaire du conscience, qui ne se commande pas"—religion is a matter of conscience which cannot be ordered. The Bible, as well as the above-mentioned principle "compelle intrare," should be interpreted in accordance with "la Lumière Naturelle"—natural reason, which rejects forced conversion and commands religious toleration because of the difficulty of ascertaining the nature of truth. He believed that Christians, Jews, and Moslems should enjoy mutual religious toleration because no one can claim absolute knowledge of God's commands and of the ultimate mysteries of the universe. As to the Augustinian justification of using constraint, Bayle wrote, "What matters is not to which end constraint is used, but whether it is used at all."

Religion and Superstition

Francois-Marie Voltaire, the eighteenth-century French philosopher and author, in his encyclopedia (which he called a *Philosophic Dictionary*) thanked Bayle for familiarizing him with the art of doubt. Educated by Jesuits in the art of dialectic, of proving anything, he stated, "I have taken as my patron saint St. Thomas of Didymus, who always insisted on an examination with his own hands." As an illustration of Voltaire's application of the "art of doubt," one of his works (which fill ninety-nine volumes) may serve—the pamphlet called "The Questions of Zapata," in which Zapata, a candidate for the priesthood, asks: "How shall we proceed to show that the Jews, whom we burn by the hundred, were for four thousand years the chosen people of God?"

Voltaire, detesting intolerance and superstition, stressed the fundamental distinction between religion and superstition. In his articles on "God" and "Theist" in the *Dictionary*, he defends religion and expounds his faith in the existence of a supreme being "who has formed all things" and "who punishes without cruelty all crimes, and recompenses with goodness all virtuous actions." Religion, he argued, should not be confused with superstition, which he described as the "cruelest enemy of pure worship due to the Supreme Being," as "a monster which has always torn the bosom of its mother," and as "a serpent which chokes religion in its embrace" that must have its head crushed "without wounding the mother whom it devours."

In his later life Voltaire, hostile to religious dogmatism, expended more and more of his effort to combat intolerance and injustice. The Calas case was one of the events that provoked him to his crusade to "crush the infamy" of ecclesiasticism and intolerance (he used the motto *Ecrasez l'infame* to end all his letters) by waging a relentless war against superstition, corruption, and abuses of the church. The Catholic church in his time enjoyed absolute sovereignty, and Voltaire's famous fight to secure justice for the family

of Jean Calas of Toulouse, a victim of religious persecution, stirred the soul of France, if not of Europe,
on behalf of tolerance, liberty, and humanity.

Jean Calas, who followed the profession of a mer-
chant in Toulouse for over forty years, was known
as a good parent and a respected citizen. He, his wife,
and all his children (one son, Louis Calas, excepted)
were Protestants. For thirty years, a maid-servant, a
zealous Catholic, brought up all his children. One
of his sons, Marc-Antonio, who could not as a Protestant enter into business nor be admitted to the bar
as a lawyer, hanged himself—presumably because of
the disappointments he had experienced. When the
people of Toulouse gathered in crowds about the
house, some fanatic in the mob cried out that Jean
Calas had hanged his own son. In consequence, a
rumor started in Toulouse—a city that celebrated by
annual procession and bonfire the Massacre of St.
Bartholomew (when four thousand Huguenots were
massacred as heretics)—that the father had killed
the son to prevent his imminent conversion to
Catholicism.

Calas was arrested and sentenced to be broken on
the wheel. His son Pierre was shut up in a monastery
of Dominicans; the daughters were taken from their
mother and shut up in a convent. The daughters were
restored to their mother only after three famous law-
yers took up the widow's cause. Voltaire, in his
"Treatise on Tolerance," concludes the account of
the death of Jean Calas by pointing out that "the
abuse of the most holy religion has produced a great
crime. It is therefore to the interest of mankind to
examine if religion should be charitable or savage."

The Calas case was only one of the tyrannous injustices resulting from fanaticism composed of superstition and ignorance that Voltaire opposed.

In the article on "Tolerance" in his *Philosophical Dictionary*, Voltaire asks why the same men who in private admit indulgence, benevolence, and justice, in public rise up so furiously against these virtues. Because, he maintains, men who "enrich themselves with the spoils of the poor, fatten themselves with his blood, and laugh at his imbecility . . . detest tolerance, as contractors enriched at the expense of the public are afraid to open their accounts, and as tyrants dread the name of liberty."

Although, according to Voltaire, Christians have been the most intolerant of all men, he nevertheless believed that of all religions, "the Christian ought doubtless to inspire the most tolerance." Because of the horrible discord experienced by mankind for so many centuries, Voltaire appealed for mutual forgiveness because "discord is the great evil of the human species, and toleration is its only remedy." He defined tolerance as "the portion of humanity" and as "the first law of nature."

Separation of Government from Church

John Locke (1632–1704), the English philosopher called the "founder of British Empiricism" who greatly influenced Voltaire, proclaimed toleration as "the chief characteristic mark of the Church." He, like Voltaire, believed that freedom of religion is a natural right that neither any single person, nor churches, nor governments have any just title to invade. He wrote three essays in favor of religious toleration. In his *A Letter Concerning Toleration,* Locke appealed to the conscience of those who upon pretense of religion persecute, destroy, starve, and maim men with corporal punishment to make them Christians and procure their salvation. Nobody will ever believe, he maintained, that such torments can proceed from charity, love, and goodwill. This "burning zeal for God," stated Locke, is "contrary to the glory of God, to the purity of the Church" and is "diametrically opposite to the profession of Christianity."

The only remedy, according to Locke, to put an end to controversy is the separation of civil government from the church. The interest of men's souls should be distinguished from the interest of the commonwealth. Religion is a matter of faith, and the nature of faith is that it cannot be compelled to the belief of anything by outward force. The power of true religion consists "in the inward and full persuasion of the mind, and faith is not faith without believing." God has never given the authority to take care of souls to one man over another or to compel anyone to his religion. Locke went a step further by stating that such power cannot be vested in the state even by the consent of the people, because no man can abandon the care of his own salvation. No man can leave the choice of his faith to any other, and "no man can prescribe to another what faith or worship he shall embrace."

Locke argued that nobody is born a member of any church. Since the church is "a society of members voluntarily uniting to that end," joining the church should be absolutely free and spontaneous. The only business of the church, according to Locke, is the salvation of souls. No one can be saved by a religion he distrusts or by worship he abhors. "Faith only, and inward sincerity, are the things that procure acceptance with God." Imposition of religion upon any people contrary to their own judgment "is in effect to command them to offend God. . . ." If we are not fully satisfied in our own mind with the worship to which we conform, we add to other sins "those also of hypocrisy, and contempt of His Divine Majesty." The ecclesiastical authority of the Church ought to be confined within its bounds, and it cannot in any manner be extended to civil affairs, "because the Church itself is a thing absolutely separate and distinct from the commonwealth."

The "commonwealth" is defined by Locke as "a society of men constituted only for processing, preserving, and advancing their own civil interests." The civil interests include life, liberty, and property. The civil power of the government ("the magistrate") is confined to the care of promoting the "civil interests," and it cannot and ought not in any manner be extended to the salvation of souls. Princes, wrote Locke, are "born superior unto other men in power, but in nature equal." Therefore, neither the right nor the art of ruling carries with it the knowledge of true religion. Thus, like Bayle and Voltaire, Locke introduces the principle of uncertainty about true religion as fundamental to the promotion of religious toleration.

Religious tolerance, stated Locke, does not permit the government to prejudice any man in the enjoyment of his civil rights because of his religion. All his civil rights and franchises that belong to him are inviolably preserved to him. "No violence nor injury is to be offered him, whether he be Christian or Pagan." Since the power of civil government relates only to men's civil rights, it is confined "to the care of the things of this world, and hath nothing to do with the world to come." In other words, the boundaries on both sides, on the side of the church as well as on the side of the state, are fixed and immovable.

Political Tolerance

The influence of Locke was exceedingly great. It spread widely in eighteenth-century Europe, and it has been asserted that all the philosophy of that century stemmed from him. Locke's ideas on natural law contributed to the beginning of a new social and economic system that reflected the meaning of newborn ideas of freedom of religion and of thought and of a government limited in its powers and based firmly on consent. Locke's conception of a fiduciary relation between free individuals and rulers with the duties of the government as trustee and with the rights of the community as beneficiary was appealing to those who struggled for the preservation of the independence, freedom, and equality with which individuals are endowed by nature.

Locke's conception of religious tolerance, based on the separation of church and state and on the religious freedom of the individual, was a landmark in the history of relations between government and the church, which in England from the time of the Tudors had backed the claims of monarchy. His doctrine of the separation of powers, although not formulated as clearly as by Montesquieu or as by modern practice (which places the legislative, executive, and judicial functions in distinct hands, while Locke's thought permitted combining them), and his doctrine of consent between government and society were the main sources of the English Revolution of 1688 (the so-called "Glorious Revolution"), of the ideas that underlay the American Revolution of 1776, and of the traditions of political tolerance that emerged in the nineteenth and twentieth centuries. This tradition of political tolerance made possible the rise of the modern political party.

The system of governance through political parties arose in Great Britain, beginning in the seventeenth century. The oppositions which gave birth to the parties were initially religious. The Anglicans, who favored the Established church and supported the power of the king, grew into the Tory party. The Dissenters, Protestants who belonged to sects other than the Established church and who upheld the power of the Parliament, were labeled Whigs. These divisions were often social and economic as well. The Tories were stronger in rural areas and were favored by the country gentlemen. The Whigs, more numerous in urban areas, tended to be strong among the new mercantile middle class.

Although the British parties first arose in the seventeenth century, these distinctions continued to be important throughout subsequent British political history. After the French Revolution, the Whig party espoused political and social reforms that culminated in the passage of the Reform Bill of 1832.

About that time, the name "Tory" gave way to "Conservative," and the name "Whig" to "Liberal." In the era of Benjamin Disraeli, his followers called themselves "young Tories" and ultraconservatives were referred to as Tories. In the twentieth century, the line of division between the Tories and the Whigs became outmoded and gave way to new groupings of contestants. The two principal parties of today are the Conservative party (which like the Tories appeals to the gentry and the upper middle class) and the Labor party (which appeals to organized labor and the lower middle class). Minor third parties may on occasion hold the balance of powers.

As the parties first arose, their coexistence was not based on ideas of political tolerance. Nor was that coexistence a peaceful one. The execution of King Charles I, the reign of his son Charles II after the Restoration of the monarchy (marked by a gradual increase in parliamentary power and the rise of political parties), and the so-called Glorious Revolution of 1688 (in which James II, who succeeded his brother Charles II, was forced to abdicate in favor of his daughter Mary and her husband, William) were all tremendous upheavals in an age fraught with religious plotting and violence. These successive upheavals were only in part caused by a fear of the monarchs' leaning toward Catholicism, a religion which neither of the incipient parties was willing to tolerate officially.

The ultimate issue was the supremacy in government of either the King or Parliament. Charles I (1600–1649), who lost the bitter struggle with the Parliament, was tried, condemned to death, and beheaded. This struggle, known as the Puritan Revolution, marked the emergence of the middle class—the new bourgeois class, Calvinist by inclination. This group perennially suspected the monarchy of having plans to restore Roman Catholicism in England, and finally these suspicions were brought to a head by James II. He was deposed without bloodshed in 1688 (in the Glorious Revolution, so named because of its peacefulness in contradistinction to the Puritan Revolution, with its warlike violence and its regicide). The joint coronation of William and Mary to replace James II ultimately established the supremacy of Parliament in the English government.

Political Parties

The party system, however, did not become a decisive part of government in Great Britain until the nineteenth century, when Parliament—by then representing a much more widely enfranchised electorate—gained final ascendancy over the monarch as the ruling body of the nation. Each party became an organized body within itself, with an internal structure and an effective means of disciplining its members into a cohesive group within Parliament. (Party discipline in Great Britain is much stronger than in the United States, where legislators seldom vote strictly along party lines except for purposes of organizing the houses of Congress and their Committees).

One British historian pointed out the relationship between the British party system and the tradition of political tolerance which underpins the British system of government:

> "Tolerance in this country is a principle of long standing. It has developed gradually from the struggles of the seventeenth century. It has been carried out in the laws; but it is still more an attitude of mind. It is, however, not tolerance alone that makes democratic government work. With us, the majority is not permanent. . . . Majorities are unstable, and the Opposition of today is the Government of tomorrow. This important fact must not be forgotten, for it enables the minority to submit peacefully and even cheerfully to the fulfillment of the policy of the majority." (W. Ivor Jennings, *The British Constitution*, Cambridge University Press, 1942, pp. 32–33.)

The important part of the British system of government referred to as "His (or Her) Majesty's Opposition" dramatizes the need for tolerance of diverse opinions. In the seventeenth century, it was the function of the Parliament to oppose the King. Now it is the function of "His Majesty's Opposition" to oppose the governmental majority. The Leader of the opposition has a shadow Cabinet that formulates a rival policy to that of the government in power. He has a salary paid from public funds included in each year's appropriation. The opposition, which always presents the electorate with the possibility of an alternative government, is as loyal as the government in power to the British system of government. In both World Wars, for instance, it shared responsibility by

becoming a part of the wartime coalition governments. At the end of the wars, the coalitions broke
up, and the political parties appealed for the voters
of the electorate. Even under normal circumstances,
the government in power in Great Britain must take
into account the views of the opposition, which functions together with the majority government as guar-
dians of the British tradition of parliamentary
government.

Jefferson's Impact on Tolerance

Locke, as we mentioned, had an impact not only
on the British system of government but also on the
ideals of the American Revolution of 1776. He greatly
influenced Thomas Jefferson, and the infusion of the
idea of natural rights with the spirit of natural law
found its expression in our Declaration of Independence. Jefferson, like Locke, believed that "man,
being the workmanship of the omnipotent and
infinitely wise Maker," has rights on his own to freedom of religion. The importance of religious tolerance in the United States may be traced back to
Jefferson's defense of religious freedom. In his *Notes
on Virginia*, 1782, Jefferson wrote:

> "Reason and free enquiry are the only effectual
> agents against error. . . . It is error alone which
> needs the support of government. Truth can
> stand by itself. . . . Difference of opinion is ad-
> vantageous in religion. . . . Is uniformity attain-
> able? Millions of innocent men, women and
> children since the introduction of Christianity

have been burnt, tortured, fined, imprisoned. Yet have we not advanced one inch towards uniformity. What has been the effect of coercion? To make one half the world fools and the other half hypocrites. To support roguery and error all over the earth. . . ."

Jefferson saw in reason and free inquiry "the natural enemies of error" and was determined to destroy the alliance between the church and the state as the barrier to free inquiry and as the enemy of personal freedom. This determination was supported by the peace and order enjoyed by the states of Pennsylvania and New York that had long subsisted without an establishment of state religion at all. The result of this experiment, witnessed by Jefferson, was not religious dissension, but an unparalleled harmony that could be ascribed to nothing but the "unbounded tolerance" of these two states that silenced religious disputes.

To protect his fellow citizens in Virginia from coercion in matters of conscience and to proclaim their right to worship as they chose, Jefferson drafted a Bill for Establishing Religious Freedom that advocated full religious liberty. Following the sweeping declaration that Almighty God had created man free and that all attempts to influence him by punishment tend "only to beget habits of hypocrisy" and are departures "from the plan of the holy author of our religion," the Bill provided

"that no man shall be compelled to frequent or support any religious worship, place, or ministry whatsoever, nor shall be enforced, restrained, molested, or burthened in his body or goods, nor shall otherwise suffer on account of his religious opinions or beliefs but that all men shall be free to profess, and by argument to maintain, their opinions in matters of religion, and that the same shall in no wise diminish, enlarge, or affect their civil capacities. . . ."

Because of the opposition of the General Assembly of Virginia, the Bill waited several years for passage. When at last it had been approved, Jefferson, who was at that time in France, wrote to Madison, "It is honorable for us to have produced the first legislation which had the courage to declare that the reason of man may be trusted with the formation of his opinions."

Locke's influence was not confined to ideas of religious tolerance. Into the political texture of American life are interwoven the ideas of English constitutionalism of which Locke was a prominent spokesman. Our republican type of representative democracy was created in the image of the English representative ideal, to which Locke had given expression, claiming that "The end of government is the good of mankind." This type of democracy provided a climate for the cultivation of political tolerance, but the distinctive source of political tolerance in the United States was the unity and the identity of purposes of the early settlers who came to America with the aim of building a society that would offer its members equality of opportunity with little political control. This identity of purpose embraced both conservatives and liberals. Moreover, the tradition of tolerance was indispensable in order to accomplish another unique purpose of the American experiment in establishing equality in freedom: to stimulate similar aspirations of other nations.

Jefferson, in his belief that the "eyes of the virtuous all over the earth are turned with anxiety on us, as the only depositories of the sacred fire of liberty," saw in "a just and solid republican government . . . a standing monument and example for the aim and imitation of the people of other countries." On a similar note President Lincoln stressed that the Declaration of Independence gave liberty "not alone to the people of this country, but hope to the world for all future time." Only political tolerance could guarantee that America would never become an image of Europe, where intolerance under the pretext of public safety was a tool used by corrupted governments to enhance the heresy that man is incapable of self-government.

Opposing Political Ideas

Tolerance, which constituted the fundamental prerequisite for the success of the American experiment, did not imply conformity of thought and of the conceptions concerning national purpose and the ways to achieve it. Tolerance permitted the expression of diametrically opposed political ideas. We shall mention only two such contradictory conceptions. One related to foreign policy: Charles Pinckney (1746 –1825), the American statesman and diplomat, declared on January 25, 1787, at the Federal Convention, of which he was a member, that "we mistake the object of our government, if we hope or wish it is to make us respectable abroad." Following the Greek philosophers, he saw the purpose of the new nation in the good life, in which foreign policy could largely be neglected. Alexander Hamilton represented an opposite point of view when on June 29 of the same year he declared, "No Government could give us tranquility and happiness at home, which did not possess sufficient stability and strength to make us respectable abroad." Hamilton followed the European tradition that expected the government to obtain not only domestic tranquility but also respectability in the eyes of foreign nations.

One of the controversies as old as American politics was the argument of a strong versus a weak federal government. The two contrasting political groups were represented by Jefferson and Hamilton. Both were openly antagonistic members of Washington's Cabinet, and Washington was unable to reconcile them. Jefferson, born of the highest aristocracy of Virginia, had a passionate love of liberty and a faith in the people's capacity for self-government. In his zeal as an apostle of agrarian democracy, Jefferson saw his ideal in a community of independent families solidly established in their farms, self-subsistent and needing little or no interference. "Those who labor in the earth are the chosen people of God, if ever he had a chosen people." A strong centralized government by its nature could endanger liberty. Hamilton, a self-made man in the fullest sense, saw in the federal government an indispensable tool for an ordered society and for the collective interests of the people. He and James Madison provided the leadership in securing the adoption of the Constitution.

Jefferson saw in government a horde of office-holders dominated by greed and corruption, depriving free individuals of the fruits of their labor on their God-given land in this blessed country of the United States. Hamilton did not find in Jefferson's faith in the free expression of the individual an assurance of man's capacity to deal on his own with the conflicting interests arising in a society without some kind of direction in public affairs, which only a government with a strong central authority can provide. He feared that a weak government would lead to disunion and anarchy.

The opposing philosophies of the two men have continued to influence the political history of the United States. Hamilton was the recognized leader of those who favored the Constitution and who called themselves the Federalists. The Anti-Federalists, who earned this name because they fought desperately against the ratification of the Constitution, feared that the Constitution would provide too strong and too centralized a government. With the loss of the battle, in order to restrict the powers of the new national government, they chose their own interpretation of the Constitution, accepted Jefferson as their leader, and identified themselves as Jeffersonian Republicans. Their aim was to destroy forever the possibility of a monarchy or of an aristocratic government. Acting as champions for the oppressed, they advocated a wider distribution of wealth, thus gaining strength among the destitute immigrants arriving in this country.

The Republicans were the origin of the present Democratic party. (The irony is that President Reagan became the modern promulgator of anti-governmental Jeffersonianism.) Jefferson did not call himself either a Federalist or an anti-Federalist. He was anxious to preserve the unity and cooperation of the new government and claimed, "We are all Republicans, we are all Federalists."

There was animosity between Jefferson and Hamilton and their followers. They became openly antagonistic, but both of them shared the same passion—they loved their country above all things. When in the presidential election Aaron Burr was found to have tied in number of votes with Jefferson, the choice of a President was thrown into the House of Representatives. After a long deadlock, Jefferson was elected, largely because Hamilton advised Federalists to support Jefferson. This election marked a historical triumph of political tolerance. For the first time in the modern era, the reins of the government were peacefully transferred by popular election from a governing party (the Federalists with President John Adams retiring from public life) to an opposition (Jefferson and his Republicans).

The System of Party Government

The party system in the United States grew indirectly out of the British experience in the eighteenth century. In the colonial period, the early Americans were divided, as in Britain, into two opposed groups, the Tories and the Whigs. The first favored the crown and represented the merchants, large landowners, and commercial creditors. The Whigs advocated home rule and voiced the sentiments of the indebted inland farmers. The conflicting interests of opposing groups did not imply a two-party system. The Federalists, for instance, saw themselves as defenders of the Constitution and not as a party. Similarly, Jefferson's attitude toward the party system was characteristic of that of other early American leaders; he profoundly distrusted party politics and was uncomfortable in admitting the role party actually came to play in American political life, even in its earliest years. For John Adams, our first vice president, the division of the Republic into two great parties "is to be feared as the greatest political evil under the Constitution." The frequent splits and formation of new parties did not enhance the popularity of a party system.

Even in spite of the fact that the Founding Fathers looked with mistrust at the party system, the United States evolved a system of party government that has been one of the bulwarks of liberty in the nation. One of the principal qualities developed by the party system in the United States, as in Great Britain, is the atmosphere of mutual tolerance, resulting in the tradition of responsible opposition engaged in a legitimate activity, and of adherence to the rules of constitutional procedure and of fairness. The spirit of political tolerance is sustained in years of election when the political chips are piled high and the campaigns tend to inflame the participants. No punitive action is taken by the winners against those who opposed them. Any attempt to transcend the bounds of what is legal, moral, and civil will turn the momentum in favor of the opposition.

In the United States, the common belief in political tolerance is strengthened by the common ground on which the two parties stand. Neither of the two political parties has a doctrinaire set of principles that stand in fierce opposition to those of the other party. The lines of distinction between the platforms of the two parties are not clearly drawn. No meaningful differences are to be found in the ultimate goals sought by the two parties. The distinction rather appears in the role assigned by the parties to the government in achieving those goals. The Democrats have a tendency to use the government for furnishing social services on a wider scale than the Republicans, who place greater faith in private initiative and in the individual's ability to shape his destiny. Bipartisan consensus often reflects the general agreement on a broad range of issues in foreign policy and other important matters faced by our nation.

In a time of crisis in the United States, for instance, the President will usually invite to the White House the Congressional leaders of both parties to inform them of the situation at hand and to seek their advice and cooperation. At the moments of greatest importance, the cooperation is often greatest. In 1948, for instance, when the United States was embarking on the then-momentous step of entering into the North American Treaty Organization (NATO), it was a Republican Senator, Arthur H. Vandenberg, who introduced into the Congress the resolution that made it possible for the Democratic President, Harry S. Truman, to pursue the ends of the treaty. Although the lack of clear party lines and strong party discipline in our country may be somehow confusing, it is a pattern that has served well to prevent the more doctrinaire multiparty system and to accept tolerance as the fundamental principle of our democracy.

Political Diversity in Democracy

The term "democracy" was originated in Greece to describe a government where people participate in directing the affairs of the State and in making its laws. Pure democracy, however, did not exist in Greece. There was always an aristocratic or oligarchic basis for representation in the State. The masses could only claim the power of criticism and judgment of the government's policies and conduct. For Plato, the participation of the masses in government, which in extreme form becomes mob rule, and the principles advocated by democracy, which include equality of rights and freedom of speech, were only sources of evil. Plato rejected democracy, while Aristotle accepted it as a lesser evil. Where we have mob rule, stated Aristotle, we have demagogues: "For in cities governed democratically, but also legally, there are no demagogues: the best among the citizens take the lead." He warned that when "demagogues come into play" democracy turns into tyranny.

The chief distinction that sets democracy apart from totalitarian regimes is that it requires from its citizens and leaders tolerance of political diversity. Without tolerance, while permitting citizens to formulate their preferences, majority rule degenerates into a tyranny that imposes on them an oppressive yoke of uniformity in opinion and action. Citizens should also have unimpaired opportunities to change their preferences, which may be affected by multifarious causes, some laudable, some blamable. Preferences are continually changing because questions of social or political character may have new aspects in a rapidly changing society. History shows us that opinions in a certain period are often deemed false or unreasonable in a subsequent time. It is certain that some of our present preferences will be rejected by future ages. What should never be changed, however, is the guarantee, necessary for democracy, that the freedom of the individual to express his preferences will always be preserved.

In stressing that tolerance, demanding unrestrained freedom of discussion, is essential to democracy, John Stuart Mill wrote, "If all mankind minus one were of one opinion, mankind would be no more justified in silencing that person than he, if he had the power, would be justified in silencing mankind." Mill argued that silencing the expression of an opinion is doing more harm to those who dissent from the opinion than those who hold it. "If the opinion is right, they are deprived of the opportunity of exchanging error for truth; if wrong, they lose . . . the clearer perception and livelier impression of truth produced by its collision with error."

In a democracy, the "self-government" of the people" does not mean the government of each by himself, but of each by an elective and responsible government. The will of the "people" does not mean the will of all the people but of the part of the people that succeeded in being accepted as the majority.

To protect the individual from the tyranny of the majority, the holders of power remain accountable to all the people, and only through a free exchange of ideas and free debate can the wisdom of political decisions be carefully evaluated by every member of a democratic community who has the right to vote in a free and fair election.

Our representative form of government precludes "mob rule," or widespread participation in governing in a direct sense. The people have the "equality of rights and freedom of speech," which they use in deciding to accept or to refuse the men who are to rule them. The electorate has a free choice among the would-be leaders who compete for his vote. The competition is on issues and often on personality. Political tolerance, which is crucial for the voter's judgment, demands of the candidates an explanation of their positions on issues affecting the life of the nation and the welfare of its citizens. Their positions may be unpopular, but they express them without fear of reprisal. The debates of competing candidates have become a popular scene of action in American politics.

The "great" debates started with the Lincoln-Douglas joint appearances before the American public. Slavery was the vital subject of their political arguments, which attracted crowds too great for public halls, so the two rivals met in open groves. In this generation, millions of plain Americans watched the debates between Kennedy and Nixon, Carter and Ford, Carter and Reagan, and Reagan and Mondale. The content of the debates included such issues as foreign policy, inflation, the decline of the cities, oil and energy, social security, and other propositions, all revolving around the role of government, the safety of our nation, our economic stability, and the use of American power. The televised debates brought together in one audience millions of voters so as to give them the opportunity to choose their political leaders. By their choice, they expressed indirectly their opinions on the debate issues of their concern.

Through tolerance, which permits free debate and free exchange of ideas, government becomes responsive to the will of the people. The history of tolerance is the history of the triumph of truth over intolerance and falsehood. By persecution and intolerance, truth may be withheld from disclosure at one time or at many times, but in the course of the ages we find it rediscovered, generally accepted, and resistant to further attempts to suppress it. Silencing the free exchange of ideas is an assumption of infallibility.

How Much Tolerance?

We are not infallible, democracy is not perfect, and we cannot expect even perfect tolerance. This brings us back to the question, raised at the beginning of this essay, of how much tolerance is justified to preserve a balance between tolerance and other values. What restraints can be placed on the extent of tolerance to protect society from infringing on its political liberties or rights? What are the rules of democratic restraint to prevent tolerance of intolerance from being utilized for antidemocratic purposes? When in a democracy is the government justified in prohibiting the promulgation of opinions dangerous to democracy or in restraining the right of demonstration with the purpose of undermining the foundation of public order?

The strain between tolerance and intolerance (or tolerance of intolerance) may be illustrated by two opinions of the Supreme Court—in each case, dissenting opinions from Justice Holmes and Brandeis, respectively. In the case of *Abrams v. United States* (250 U.S. 616, 617, 40 S.Ct. 17 [1919]), the defendants were charged with conspiring, when the United States was at war with Germany, to unlawfully utter, print, write, and publish "disloyal, scurrilous and abusive language about the form of government of the United States," to "incite, provoke and encourage resistance to the United States in said war," and to "incite and advocate curtailment of production of things and products necessary and essential to the prosecution of the war." After denouncing President Wilson as a hypocrite and a coward and assailing our government in general, the defendants appealed to the "workers" of this country to arise and put down by force the government of the United States as a "capitalistic enemy." The articles of the defendants contained a definite threat "to create so great a disturbance that the autocrats of America shall be compelled to keep their armies at home, and not be able to spare any for Russia." There was also a threat of armed rebellion. "If they will use arms against the Russian people to enforce their standard of order, so will we use arms, and they shall never see the ruin of the Russian Revolution."

The Supreme Court affirmed the judgment of the District Court for the Southern District of New York convicting the defendants of conspiring to violate provisions of the Espionage Act of Congress (of June 15, 1917, as amended by the Act of May 16, 1918). The plain purpose of their criminal conduct, stated the Court, was "to excite, at the supreme crisis of war, disaffection, sedition, riots, and, they hoped, revolution in this country for the purpose of embarrassing and if possible defeating the military plans of the government in Europe."

Justice Holmes in his dissent argued that the principle of the right to free speech is always the same, even against charges peculiar to war. "It is only the present danger of immediate evil or an intent to bring it about that warrants Congress in setting a limit to the expression of opinion where private rights are not concerned. . . . Now nobody can suppose that the surreptitious publishing of a silly leaflet by an unknown man, without more, would present any immediate danger that its opinions would hinder the success of the government arms or have any appreciable tendency to do so." (250 U.S. 616, 628, 40 S.Ct. 17, 21 [1919].)

This lack of consensus over the direction of public policy and over a definition of the limits of tolerance appeared also in the case of *Gitlow v. People of the State of New York*. Benjamin Gitlow was indicted for the statutory crime of criminal anarchy as defined by the New York Penal Code. The judgment was affirmed by the Court of Appeals. The defendant, a member of the Left Wing Section of the Socialist Party, advocated in a published "Manifesto" the destruction of the state and the establishment of the dictatorship of the proletariat by "organizing the industrial proletariat into militant Socialist unions and at the earliest opportunity through mass strike and force and violence, if necessary, compelling the government to cease to function, and then through a proletarian dictatorship, taking charge of and appropriating all property. . . ." (268 U.S. 652, 662, 45 S.Ct. 625, 628 [1925].)

The Supreme Court affirmed the judgment of the Court of Appeals that held that the Manifesto "advocated the overthrow of the government by violence, or by unlawful means." It is a fundamental principle, stated the Supreme Court, that the freedom of speech and of the press "does not confer an absolute right to speak or publish, without responsibility, whatever one may choose, or an unrestricted and unbridled license that gives immunity for every possible use of language and prevents the punishment of those who abuse this freedom." Freedom of speech and of the press does not protect publications promoting the overthrow of the government by force or teachings which tend to subvert the government or to hinder it in the performance of its duties. The State, according to the Supreme Court, is the primary judge of regulations required in the interest of public safety and welfare, and its statutes may be declared unconstitutional only when they are arbitrary and unreasonable.

Justice Holmes, in his dissenting opinion, agreed that the test sanctioned by the full Court in *Schenck v. United States* (249 U.S. 47, 52, 39 S.Ct. 247, 249 [1919]) applied in this case. The often-reiterated "clear and present danger" test is whether the words are used in such circumstances and are of such a nature as to create a clear and present danger that they will bring about the substantive evils that the State has a right to prevent. In Holmes' judgment, "If in the long run the beliefs expressed in proletarian dictatorship are destined to be accepted by the dominant forces of the community, the only meaning of free speech is that they should be given their chance and have their way." (*Gitlow v. People of the State of New York*, 268 U.S. 652, 673, 45 S.Ct. 625, 632 [1925].) Furthermore, the publication of the Manifesto, he stated, did not attempt to induce an uprising against the government at once but at some indefinite time in the future, and, therefore, it was too remote from possible consequences.

Necessary Measures

What is the main point of the differences in opinions on tolerance expressed above, differences that may have great consequences for the preservation of our democratic form of government? History shows us that utterances inciting the overthrow of an organized, duly elected government may kindle a spark that while smoldering for a time may break open with sudden violence into a sweeping and destructive fire. The Supreme Court has taken the position that the State cannot reasonably be required to measure the danger from every such utterance "in the nice balance of a jeweler's scale." The State is not acting arbitrarily or unreasonably when it takes measures necessary to extinguish this spark without waiting until it blazes into a conflagration.

As the Illinois Supreme Court explained in another case, *People v. Lloyd* (304 Ill. 23, 35, 136 N.E. 501, 512), the State has the authority to forbid the advocacy of a doctrine intended to overthrow the government without waiting until there is a present and imminent danger of the success of the advocated plan. "If the State were compelled to wait until the apprehended danger became certain, then its right to protect itself would come into being simultaneously with the overthrow of the government, when there would be neither prosecuting officers nor courts for the enforcement of the law."

For Justice Holmes, the danger of bringing about the "substantive evil" must be present and imminent and not too "remote from possible consequences." His dissenting opinions, quoted above, do not reflect the legal pragmatism advocated by Holmes, a pragmatism that was the prominent feature of his great work, *The Common Law*. Holmes rejected the concept of abstract justice when he wrote "that the Common Law is not a brooding omnipresence in the sky" and "the U.S. is not subject to the mystic over-law that it is bound to obey." Because of the "felt necessities," he stated, the right of free speech must be denied to a mischievous person falsely crying "Fire" in a crowded theatre and should be limited in time of war.

Adhering to the historic school of jurisprudence, he wrote:

> "The life of the law has not been logic: it has been experience. The felt necessities of the time, the

prevalent moral and political theories, intuitions of public policy, avowed or unconscious, even the prejudices which judges share with their fellow-men have had a good deal more to do than the syllogism in determining the rules by which men should be governed. . . . The substance of the law at any given time pretty nearly corresponds, so far as it goes, with what is then understood to be convenient." (*The Common Law*, Little, Brown, and Company, 1881, p. 5.)

As a pragmatist Holmes urged others to face realistically the political and social problems in a rapidly changing society. Obviously, when writing in 1919 and 1925 his dissenting opinions in the cases of *Abrams* and *Gitlow*, which we have been discussing, he could not foresee how deep human depravity brought on by communism and nazism could go. Nor did the Supreme Court give consideration to the extent of this depravity by making a distinction in numerous cases between mere advocacy of forcible overthrow of government and preparing a group for violent action or steeling it to such action.

Faith in the Democratic Process

In the perspective of historical developments and of the tragedies the world has experienced under the yoke of totalitarian regimes, the conclusion to be reached is: A democratic State should exercise its police power to punish those who abuse freedom of speech and of the press by utterance tending to disturb public peace and order, to corrupt public morals, and to incite to crime. The democratic State has the duty to protect its primary and essential right of preservation and has the authority to judge the regulations required in the interest of public safety and welfare. In our independent courts was vested the responsibility to resist every unreasonable encroachment upon the rights of the individual stipulated for in the Constitution by its declaration of rights. Due process protects the individual against arbitrary and capricious actions of the government.

This conclusion is also pertinent to the question of what restraints should be placed on the extent of tolerance to protect the public from the abuse of the right of the people "peaceably" to assemble. It is the authority of the State or the local government, which represent the free choice of democratic and law-abiding citizens, to prevent or punish where "clear and present danger" of rioting, burning, looting, and of any other public disorder appears or presents an immediate threat to peace and public safety. States and cities should be sustained in this power in order for the people not to lose faith in the democratic process of free choice of their governments. Freedom of assembly exists under the law and not independently of it.

The strategy of mass demonstrations as used by groups resorting to terror tactics was summed up by Hitler: "We should not work in secret conventicles but in mighty mass demonstrations, and it is not by dagger and poison or pistol that the road can be cleared for the movement but by the conquest of the streets." (Quoted from Justice Jackson's dissenting opinion in *Terminiello v. City of Chicago*, 337 U.S. 1, 23,

69 S.Ct. 894, 904 [1949].) Our constitutional rights will be endangered if we do not have protection from abuses which lead to violence and destruction. The rights of free speech and assembly do not mean that everyone with opinions and beliefs has the right to say what he pleases or to engage in demonstrations where he pleases and when he pleases. It is a myth to consider such rights as constitutional.

Civil liberty does not mean removal of all restraints from those who abuse this liberty and advocate the evil of intolerance. It cannot be stressed enough, however, that the power to prevent any conduct which induces people to violate the law cannot be invoked in bad faith, as a cover for suppression or censorship, which is in direct conflict with the kind of government envisioned by those who adopted our Bill of Rights. The holders of power remain always accountable to their communities. In a democracy, the people demand from their governments a policy of tolerance, since communication with one another and exchange of ideas constitute the basis of all common achievement.

Democracy flourishes in a free market of ideas where truth gets itself accepted in the competition provided by the free trade of ideas visualized by the Framers of the Constitution. Society must, therefore, be vigorously protected against self-appointed "heralds of truth" who can do to the public as much or more harm as if the allegedly harmful ideas they are trying to suppress are tolerated. In diversity of opinion, stated John Stuart Mill, is the only "chance of a fair play to all sides of the truth." Free discussion cannot be denied, and the right of criticism must not be stifled. The worst offense which can be committed by a polemic "is to stigmatize those who hold the contrary opinion as bad and immoral men."

In my book *Three Sources of National Strength*, I listed tolerance as one of the important elements of patriotism. I pointed out that one of the abuses of patriotism is to use it as a club to attack fellow citizens who differ in their opinions from oneself. The welfare of our society is endangered when those who proclaim themselves patriots attack the patriotism of faithful public servants and irresponsibly attempt to destroy the harmony of society by seeing treason in all dissidence. The deepest sense of patriotism is betrayed by those who by self-assertion, belligerence, and hatred impugn the motives of others. I wrote,

> "If one claims that his opinion is the voice of God and condemns all whose opinions differ from his own, then God has actually been left out of the picture. . . . Mutual tolerance is the inner light in which freedom lives and grows, it is the air from which man draws the breath of love for his country." (The University of Texas at Dallas, 1986, p. 148.)

Arthur Miller, in a note to the first act of *The Crucible*, emphasizes the danger in irresponsible suppression of dissidence:

> "In the countries of the Communist ideology, all resistance of any import is linked to the totally malign capitalist succubi, and in America any man who is not reactionary in his views is open

to the charge of alliance with the Red hell. Political opposition, thereby, is given an inhumane overlay which then justifies the abrogation of all normally applied customs of civilized intercourse. A political policy is equated with moral right, and opposition to it with diabolical malevolence. Once such an equation is effectively made, society becomes a congeries of plots and counterplots, and the main role of government changes from that of the arbiter to that of the scourge of God." (Viking Press, 1954, p. 34.)

Our nation has repeatedly struggled against the forces of intolerance. History reminds us that in the United States intolerance—manifesting itself in the garb of loyalty, with all its attendant overzealous partisanship and witch-hunting—was behind the infamous Alien and Sedition Laws of 1798 (the Alien Law passed on June 25 and the Sedition Law on July 14, but usually they are named together), the Sedition Act of 1918, and the so-called McCarthy period (1950–1954). The infamous Alien and Sedition Laws of 1798 passed because of the fear that French Liberalism and an alliance between the French and the leaders of the Republican Party would endanger the Federalist party's programs.

The Alien Act gave the President power to banish from the country any alien whom he judged suspicious, without giving a reason and without conducting a trial of any sort. The Sedition Act made it a crime, punishable by fine and imprisonment, to be found guilty of "combining and conspiring to oppose the execution of the laws, or publishing false or malicious writings against the President, Congress, or the government of the United States." The Sedition Act was aimed chiefly at Republican newspapers.

President Adams made no use of the law empowering him to expel dangerous aliens and the Alien Law was never enforced; it expired unused two years after its enactment. Not so with the Sedition Act. The arrest of editors who criticized the government proved to be a boomerang to the Federalists. The Sedition Act, intended to release partisan bitterness, helped to unite the opposition and unified the party that had framed it. The Republicans, as their answer, drafted the Kentucky and Virginia Resolutions, which were designed to awake the people to the fact that the Alien and Sedition Acts were unconstitutional, since the government had overstepped its rightful authority in passing them. The Federalist party suffered a defeat in the presidential election, and when Jefferson took office in 1801, he pardoned all who were prisoners under the Sedition Law.

The doctrine of sedition was revived by the Sedition Act of 1918, which extended the offenses covered by the Espionage Act of 1917 so as to cover disloyal utterances against the government, the Constitution, the military uniform, or the flag, and went far toward abolishing freedom of speech and the press. The Postmaster General was given arbitrary power to exclude from the mail publications which seemed to violate the provisions of the sedition laws. A generation later, the so-called McCarthy period marked as targets of a witch-hunt persons suspected of disloyal intentions; such a moral climate did not generate patriotic fervor and loyalty but only intensified mutual suspicion.

As we have seen, over the years important Supreme Court decisions have discouraged attempts to constitutionalize intolerance under the guise of protecting loyalty by greatly reducing the range of constitutionally valid legislation aimed at punishing alleged disloyalty. The Court has repeatedly stressed that the liberty protected by the Constitution may not be interfered with, under the guise of protecting the public interest, by legislative action which is arbitrary or without reasonable relation to some purpose within the competency of the government to effect.

Tolerance is an indispensable quality in a democracy since it enables people of different origins, races, and religions to live together and to work together in the spirit of building an orderly society. Tolerance is a powerful medicine in a society built on the premises of individual dignity, freedom of choice, and the right to criticize public men and measures—as long as the means used are peaceful. Discord is not a sign of weakness but of strength, a sign of meaningful participation of the citizenry in the political process. Such participation must not be required to meet arbitrary standards of acceptability. We should be eternally vigilant against attempts to restrain open debate from challenging deep-seated beliefs because of fear of resentment.

Tolerance opens broader enduring values than the ones offered by "sacred" patterns dictated by those who claim a monopoly of rectitude and righteousness. A democratic society grows in wisdom by constant scrutiny of thought and ideas, and as it grows in capacity for liberty, the spirit of tolerance will grow in its citizens.

CHAPTER 3

LOYALTY

The Concept of Loyalty

Loyalty is an ethical principle essential to moral life. It may be defined as a devotion to a cause marked by thoroughness, fidelity, constancy, a sense of just purpose, and a willingness to serve. It connotes faithfulness, a duty to serve, and an allegiance to some definite authority or cause—to God, to a person, to a constitution, to a principle, or to an idea. Loyalty is not merely an affection since it demands the willingness of the loyal person to serve and to be ready to suffer as the cause demands.

Loyalty is a virtue essential to democracy since it binds the members of a society by ties that lead to unity of purpose and solidarity in service. For the American philosopher Josiah Royce, "loyalty to loyalty" is the central spirit of the moral and reasonable life of man. All the commonplace virtues, insofar as they are indeed defensible and effective, are special forms of loyalty to loyalty. "Justice, charity, industry, wisdom, spirituality, are all definable in terms of enlightened loyalty." (*The Basic Writings of Josiah Royce*, Vol. 2, University of Chicago Press, 1969, p. 860. Reprinted from *The Philosophy of Loyalty*, The Macmillan Company, 1908.)

The history of loyalty, of serving a cause beyond one's private self, is the history of human greatness—of patriots who regretted that they had but one life to give to their country, of captains standing steadfastly by their sinking ships until the last possible service could be rendered, of martyrs faithful to their religions unto death, of political prisoners who died tortured by their oppressors without betraying their freedom-seeking friends.

The fact that loyalty is a central motive in an individual's life does not mean that it affects his independent judgment, his spirit of self-assertion, or his moral autonomy. An individual's free judgment may lead him to the conclusion that his blind loyalty has been exploited for unworthy purposes. Immigrants to the United States from totalitarian countries do not hesitate to renounce their fidelity to their native countries and to pledge loyalty to this country, which offers them the right of self-expression and freedom denied to them by the oppressors who trammeled their free spirits.

A member of a political party disillusioned with the leadership of the party and with the policies adopted and consistently followed by it which conflict with his political views and moral standards may reach the conclusion that he cannot remain loyal to the ties that bound him with the other members into some sort of unity. Such a conclusion should not be interpreted as a sign of weakness or lack of fidelity. It is, rather, a sign of independence, of a refusal to become a tool in the hands of others. It is a sign of the moral autonomy of the individual, which Immanuel Kant insisted is one of our highest goods. This moral autonomy should guide the individual in determining his loyalty to any civic or social organization, club, or fraternity.

Not all causes are worthy of loyalty. There are good

and bad causes. Gangsters, mercenaries, and drug pushers also claim ties that bind them into one sort of action—criminal action. War, unless in defense against aggression, can hardly be considered a just cause. Yet loyalty has been closely associated with the activities of war. When aroused by the spirit of war, one is led to hate the enemy precisely because the enemy possesses the same personal quality of loyalty one admires in a countryman—only the enemy is loyal to a different group or cause. The ethnologist Dr. Rudolf Steinmetz of The Hague in his book *The Philosophy of War* maintained that warriors are the most typical representatives of rational loyalty. According to him, war gives an opportunity for loyal devotion so notable and important that, if war were altogether abolished, one of the greatest goods of civilization would be hopelessly lost. (Quoted in *The Basic Writings of Josiah Royce,* p. 859.)

Although it is more than doubtful whether wars do make a positive contribution to civilization, it cannot be denied that it is sometimes impossible to define what is right and what is wrong. The truth about right and wrong can be discovered only upon examination of the purpose of life. Throughout the history of mankind, prominent philosophers who have tried to discover the great truths of moral life have taken into account the importance of loyalty as one of the great virtues classifying the morality of human behavior.

Socrates, Plato, Aristotle, and Cicero

Loyalty was praised as a virtue and its importance

stressed by the ancient Greek philosophers. Socrates, condemned to death, reaffirmed his loyalty to God, to Athens, and above all to his mission to "pursue wisdom" when Crito, among other Athenians, came to his cell to advise him that a way had been found for him to escape. If he were to have left his "post" because of fear of death, he said,

> "that would have been dreadful indeed, and then in truth might I be justly brought to court for not acknowledging the existence of gods, for willful disobedience to the oracle, for fearing death, for thinking myself wise when I am not." (*Apology*, 29a, trans. by R. E. Allen, *The Dialogues of Plato*, Vol. 1, Yale University Press, 1984, p. 92.)

In his discussion with the Athenians who were visiting him in his cell, Socrates brought up the suggestion that had been made that the case against him would be dismissed on the condition that he no longer pursue his philosophy, his inquiry, and his teaching. Such conditions were in direct conflict with his loyalty to his mission:

> "If, as I say, you were to dismiss me on that condition, I would reply that I hold you in friendship and regard, Gentlemen of Athens, but I shall obey the God rather than you, and while I have breath and am able I shall not cease to pursue wisdom." (*Ibid.*, 29d.)

Socrates believed that God commanded him to persuade "young and old . . . to care not for body or money in place of, or so much as, excellence of soul." He showed himself determined to remain loyal to his true self and in his service to God, even if he had "to die for it many times over." By refusing to disobey the law and to escape, he remained loyal to the laws of the state, even if they were unjust. His choice was to die as "a victim of injustice at the hands of men" rather than to escape and trespass the law and "thus shamefully return injustice for injustice and injury for injury." (*Crito*, 54c, *The Dialogues of Plato*, p. 129.)

Plato and Aristotle both demanded unselfish loyalty and complete devotion to the city-state, the model form of social and political organization in which people participate in directing the affairs of the city *(polis)* and in making the laws. Plato in his *Laws* demanded the death penalty for any citizens found guilty of a crime committed against "the gods, or his parents, or the state." Whoever, he wrote, uses violence and is "stirring up sedition contrary to law" is the greatest enemy of the state. There should be one law for all three kinds of evildoer: "for the traitor, and the robber of temples, and the subverter by violence of the laws of the state." Every man who "is worth anything" has the obligation to inform the magistrate and "bring the conspirator to trial for making a violent and illegal attempt to change the government." The citizen who fails to discharge this obligation and the magistrate who does not suppress the man who stirs up civil strife are "nearly as bad" as the "subverter of the laws of the state." (*Laws IX*, trans. by Benjamin Jowett, *The Dialogues of Plato*, Vol. 2, Random House, 1937, pp. 600, 602.)

Plato discerned two kinds of war. One was civil war, "of all wars the worst"; the other war, with foreign nations, he classified as a "far milder form of warfare." Civil strife (of which the character Theognis speaks in the *Laws*) is a far higher test of loyalty and of man's character than foreign wars. He who is loyal in "civil broil is worth his weight in gold and silver," since he is showing all the virtues: justice, temperance, and wisdom, as well as courage. In civil strife the greatest virtue is "loyalty in the hour of danger," which "may be truly called perfect justice." Foreign wars (of which the character Tyrtacus speaks) are often fought by mercenaries who "are generally and without exception insolent, unjust, violent men, and the most sinister of human beings." Their courage ranks as a "fourth-rate" virtue after justice, temperance, and wisdom. (*Laws I*, p. 412.)

Aristotle in Book VIII of his *Nichomachean Ethics* deals with the quality called *philia* (often translated as "friendship," "harmony," or "good will"), the bond that holds the members of any association together, the bond that gives different people something in common, regardless of whether the association is a city-state, family, or business association. Aristotle's views are therefore most germane to the question of loyalty, and the term "loyalty" here, for the purpose of our discussion, may be used interchangeably with *philia*. There are three motives, according to Aristotle, that are the basis of loyalty (or friendship): usefulness, time for pleasure, and the basis of virtue or excellence. (*Nicomachean Ethics*, trans. by Martin Ostwald, Bobbs-Merrill, 1962, pp. 218–226.)

When loyalty is based only on usefulness, people "do not find joy in one another, unless they see some material advantage coming to them." The same is true of loyalty based on pleasure. Loyalty that owes its existence to these two motives disappears with the disappearance of the motives. In our time, the "loyalty" of gangsters to their boss and loyalty to tyrants or corrupted politicians will fall under this classification. When the leader of a major underworld criminal "family" is assassinated, its members will pledge loyalty to the new chief of mobsters. When a tyrant is overthrown, his palace guard or secret police will offer its services to the new dictator who spearheaded the rebellion and moved into the presidential palace. The loyalty of those who base it on utility or on pleasure dissolves as soon "as it ceases to be to their advantage, since they were friends not of one another but [of] what was profitable for them."

The perfect form of loyalty is "when people are friends on the basis of virtue or excellence." This kind of loyalty implies mutual trust and has the characteristic of being lasting. It consists in giving rather than in receiving affection. It tends to be unique, because it is impossible to extend perfect loyalty to many people or causes, just as it is impossible, stated Aristotle, "to be in love with many people at the same time. For love is like an extreme, and an extreme tends to be unique."

In their demand for loyalty to the city-state, Plato and Aristotle make a distinction between "true" and corrupt governments. The three forms of government are kingship, aristocracy, and democracy.

(Aristotle uses the term "timocracy"—government of property owners—in place of "democracy.") Of the three, states Aristotle, kingship is the best, provided that the king acts as a "shepherd of the people," looking out for his subjects. The king turns into a tyrant when he violates the laws and pursues his own good. In tyranny there is little or no place for loyalty (friendship). There is also no place for loyalty when aristocracy changes into oligarchy and the wicked rulers "take all or most things for themselves." (*Nicomachean Ethics*, p. 234).

For Plato it is possible to bisect all governments according to whether they do or do not adhere to the principles of law. Democracy may rule with law or without law. Monarchy is "divided into royalty and tyranny," and the rule of few is divided into aristocracy and oligarchy. (*The Statesman*, *The Dialogues of Plato*, p. 330.) Although democracy, according to Aristotle, is the worst of the three forms of government, he admits that of the perverted forms of government "democracy is the least wicked," since "where the citizens are equal, they have many things in common." (*Nicomachean Ethics*, pp. 236–237.)

Loyalty is not expressly mentioned by Aristotle, but it is clearly implied as a virtue of a good man whose noble actions are of benefit to his fellowman. He describes the actions that give nobility to a virtuous man's conduct as follows:

"It is also true that many actions of a man of high moral standards are performed in the interest of his friends and of his country. And if there be need, he will give his life for them. He will freely give his money, hours, and, in short, all goods, things that men compete for, while he gains nobility for himself. . . . No wonder, then, that he is regarded as a man of high moral standards, since he chooses nobility at the cost of everything else. . . ." (*Ibid.*, Book IX, pp. 262–263).

Aristotle in his treatise on *Politics* expects from the rulers, in addition to their capacity to govern, loyalty to the "State or political association" and virtue and justice compatible with the polity. In his discussion of how the well-being of the polity may best be served, he recommends education in the spirit of the polity: "Without this education the wisest laws are futile."

Plato and Aristotle in their discussion of love and devotion to the city do not bring up the problem of conflicting loyalties, for example, the conflict between loyalty to the state and personal loyalty to family members or friends. In Sophocles' *Antigone*, the classic tragedy of the remnants of the house of Oedipus, Creon, upon assuming political power in the aftermath of civil war, is faced with Antigone's act of disobedience. In the passionate debate in which Sophocles explores the issues of political expediency and conscientious objection, there is no explicit reference to loyalty, but the dilemma Antigone faces directly pertains to the conflict of loyalties. She disobeys the existing law (that no one is to bury the body of her dead brother Polyneices, since he led a war against the state) because of her two loyalties: first, her loyalty to the laws of the gods and "the lawful traditions that the gods have not written merely, but made infallible," which she does not intend to break because of "fear of one man and his principles"; and, second, her own sense of personal loyalty, which prompts her to say that "if I had let my own brother stay unburied I would have suffered all the pain I do not feel now."

Cicero undertook an analysis of conflicting loyalties to the city-state and to a friend in his *De Amicitia*. To answer the question of how far a loyalty to a friend ought to go when it conflicts with loyalty to the state, Cicero elaborates movingly on the concept of friendship. He recognizes friendship as one of the infinite ties uniting the human race and "fashioned by Nature itself." He urges people, therefore, to put friendship above all human things, for nothing is more in harmony with nature than friendship and "nothing so adaptable to our fortunes whether they be favourable or adverse." (Trans. by William Armstead Falconer, Harvard University Press, 1971, p. 127.)

Since friendship emanates directly from nature rather than from need, it must be genuine and come "of its own accord," with a feeling of love, rather than from calculation of how much profit the friendship is likely to afford. In order to obtain some advantages under the pretense of friendship, some are courted and honored "to suit the occasion; yet in true friendship there is nothing false, nothing pretended." (*Ibid.*, p. 139.)

Friendship, according to Cicero, exists only among "good men." Who are they? They are those "who so act and so live as to give proof of loyalty and uprightness, of fairness and generosity; who are free from all passion, caprice, and insolence, and have great strength of character. . . ." One of the qualities of friendship is unswerving constancy, which is obtained only through loyalty, "for nothing is constant that is disloyal. . . ." (*Ibid.*, p. 175.) What are the laws of friendship concerning the limits of loyalty when demands are made that one should do something that is wrong and dishonorable? Are, for instance, friends bound for the sake of friendship when asked to bear arms against their country?

In *De Amicitia*, this question arose in Cicero's conversation with Gaius Blossius Cumae, who came to him to plead for leniency for his support of Tiberius Gracchus, offering as a reason for a pardon that in his loyalty to Tiberius Gracchus it was his duty to do anything that Tiberius requested him. (Tiberius was a tribune and avowed reformer who passed the agrarian laws to redistribute the public land which the rich had taken over. When at election time he renominated himself, the senate declared it illegal and the election was postponed. In a riot on the following day, Tiberius was murdered.) Asked Cicero: "Even if he requested you to set fire to the Capitol?" Responded Gaius, ". . . [I]f he had I should have obeyed." (*Ibid.*, p. 149.)

Cicero found this attitude of Gaius' an ungodly one. Loyalty cannot go so far as to cause a person to commit a crime against the Republic. The first law of friendship is to do for friends only what is honorable. This law forbids one to ask a friend to perform dishonorable acts or to do them himself if asked. There is no justification to sin on behalf of a friend. In case of a conflict of loyalties, it is dishonorable for anyone to plead loyalty to a friend in defense of sin in general and especially of those sins against the state committed for "the sake of a friend." No one, according to Cicero, can argue that it is permissible to follow a friend "when waging war against his country." (*Ibid.*, pp. 151–158.)

It may be pointed out that Cicero's position was not always shared by other philosophers and writers. In the Middle Ages, Dante (1265–1321), the outstanding Italian poet and one of the great figures of world literature, in his *Divine Comedy* placed Brutus and Cassius in the lowest circle of Hell because they had chosen to betray their friend Julius Caesar rather than their country, Rome. In modern times the English novelist E. M. Forster in *Two Cheers for Democracy* deplores the fact that in our generation personal relations are "despised" and replaced by a trend to dedicate ourselves to some movement or cause. "I hate the idea of causes," wrote Forster, "and if I had to choose between betraying my country and betraying my friend, I hope I should have the guts to betray my country." (Harcourt, Brace and Company, 1951, p. 68.) I shall return to the issue of conflicting loyalties in my discussion of just purpose.

Feudal Loyalty

In the ancient writing I have been examining, loyalty finds its expression in discussions of friendship, *philia*, and love of one's country. In the Middle Ages, the basic social structure of Western Europe became the local agricultural and political economy. With this new structure came new concepts of loyalty.

With the dissolution of Charlemagne's empire and the breakdown of central government, people turned to the powerful landowners for protection. The alliance of the protector—the noble landowner—and of his subordinates grew into the feudal system. The foundation of this feudal relationship was the *fief* (which gave feudalism its name), which was usually land. The grantor of the fief was the lord, and the recipient was the vassal.

The lord granted the vassal protection and the use of land in return for personal services and duties. To acquire his fief, the vassal knelt before the lord, put his hands between the lord's hands, and swore an oath to be loyal to the lord and to perform the services and acts due to him. This was an act of homage or an act of fealty. The overlord bound himself by kissing the vassal and lifting him to his feet. By an act of investiture, he invested the vassal with the possession of the fief. The investiture called for giving to the vassal a symbol of land transferred (a straw, a clod of earth, or a stick).

There was a hierarchy of lords (knights, counts, dukes, barons, earls, and other nobles) with a series of loyalties that progressed upward from the vassal to the supreme overlord, the king. For the protection provided by the lord, the vassal had an obligation to supply a stipulated number of armed men, in addition to dues and services varying with local customs. The concentration of power into single hands by the rise of monarchies in Europe and the expansion of the economic world after the crusades broke down the feudal system by the end of the fourteenth century.

The ceremony of homage and investiture constituted a contract that hardly included the concept
of personal loyalty (a distinction should be made
here between loyalty and fealty). No personal attachment existed between the vassal and his lord that
commanded a free, devoted service to him or to a
certain cause. Fealty commanded only the respect of
faith to the pledge made by the vassal in the act of
homage to his overlord. Since it was not backed by
sentiments of personal allegiance, the contract of
feudalism offered loyalty to an office, rather than to
a person. Loyalty to the office of the king did permit resistance to an evil tyrant.

The Magna Charta—which King John was forced
to agree to because of a revolt of the barons in
1215—is the most memorable document in English
constitutional history. The "Great Charter," called
the "palladium of English liberty," gave the barons
guarantees against oppression and abuse of the
king's prerogatives. The barons exacted from King
John the commitment that he would not encroach
on their own rights and privileges. The Charter
became a symbol of the supremacy of the law of the
land over the king. Its thirty-ninth clause provides
that no free man may be "imprisoned, outlawed,
exiled, condemned, or in any way destroyed" unless
according to the law of the land.

The importance of the concessions of the Magna
Charta that were wrung from the king is that they
set forth a distinction between loyalty to the office
and loyalty to the man in the office. England became
a legal, not a regal, state. The Charter put limitations
upon the power of the king, and thus violation of any

of the articles of the Charter justified a rebellion against the king. Loyalty to the office of the king did not call for loyalty to a king who transgressed his legal powers.

Loyalty to God and Loyalty to the Church

King John was opposed not only by the barons but also by churchmen headed by Stephen Langton. The church participated in and influenced the feudal system, and some aspects of its hierarchy paralleled the feudal hierarchy. But the position of the church in society was complicated by another important concept of loyalty; in this concept, the most important loyalty was not to another individual, to a ruler, or even to the state, but to God.

A. The Hebrew Tradition

To the ancient Hebrews, the idea of loyalty was distinctly religious. They tried to please God and shrank from arousing His anger. The first four Commandments sum up duties of men toward God, and they clearly took precedence over the remaining Commandments, which summarize the duties of men toward each other. Obedience to all of them is regarded as a duty to God, the holy lawgiver. Any act of disloyalty was, therefore, sinful. Psalm 119 is an expression of the Psalmist's spirit of loyalty in his desire to fulfill the Divine Law to its end. In his inward obedience to the law of his God, he prays, "Give me understanding and I shall keep the law; Yea, I shall observe it with all my heart." He prays for help in obeying and in applying the divine law and for help in putting himself in accordance with the spirit established by God's word.

The Old and the New Testaments make a distinction between legalism and loyalty. The legalist performs his duty by not breaking the rules. The loyalist, upheld by his faith, puts his whole heart into his duty and sets no limits for fulfillment of the law. "A good man out of the good treasure of his heart bringeth that which is good." (Luke 6:45.) Israel as a whole was regarded as God's "firstborn son" (Exodus 4:22), and a man was only a fractional part of a chosen nation. When Achan sinned against God, he and his family were stoned and all their possessions burned to turn the Lord from "the fierceness of his anger" against Israel. (Joshua 7:25–26.)

The Covenant relation of Israel as a nation to Jehovah was the standard by which loyalty to God was to be judged. The nation's deference to the Covenant meant loyalty to God. (Hosea 6:7; Amos 3:1–3.) Although in the teachings of Jeremiah and Ezekiel, individual responsibility is singled out ("Every one shall die for his own iniquity," Jeremiah 31:30; Ezekiel 18:2–4), the prophets never abandoned the idea that national well-being depended upon walking "humbly with God." (Micah 6:8.)

The classical example of loyalty is the tragic offering of Isaac on the mountain of Moriah. Archeological discoveries, such as skeletons of young infants, give evidence that among the Canaanites there was a widespread custom of sacrificing the firstborn (like the first fruits or the first harvest) as sacred to divinity. Abraham, to provide his loyalty to God, sought to act according to the existing, perverted standards. Because of Abraham's readiness to sacrifice his only son, his loyalty was rewarded by the Lord's blessing. (Genesis 22:17.) Similarly, the unfailing loyalty of Jonathan, the son of Saul, to David is marked with a genuineness displayed by his efforts to save David from Saul's jealousy. The gratitude of David for Jonathan's loyalty and friendship is expressed in his eulogy on the occasion of Jonathan's death. (II Samuel 1:17–27.)

The idea of loyalty to God reaches a climax in the Book of Job. In this book a sage who has always done what the Lord required of him is afflicted with an incurable, painful malady. Because he has been afflicted with a loathsome disease, his friends abandon him and question his integrity. Yet, in all his suffering, Job holds up the lofty idea of loyalty to God's love and mercy. God's plan to discipline his followers includes suffering, which may be for the welfare of others. (Job 22:30.) This kind of allegiance to the Lord's laws and attachment to His authority in time of suffering kept the Jews together in exile.

B. The Christian Tradition

In the New Testament, communion with God can be effected only through Christ. The priesthood of Jesus removed all barriers between men and God, and loyalty to God rests on three virtues that converge in Christ: faith, hope, and love. The Mosaic law based loyalty to God on the penalty of punishment if the law is not obeyed. Jesus taught that such loyalty to God should be rendered out of love of Him and of His righteousness. Loyalty should emanate from integrity of heart and the demands of God and should be distinguished from ceremonial obligation: "Nothing that goes into a man from outside can defile him; no, it is the things that come out of him that defile a man." (Mark 7:15.) Forbearance and renunciation must be cultivated in order for a person to enter the spiritual kingdom of heaven.

After the ascendancy of Christianity to a position of worldly power during the time of Constantine, the issue of loyalty to God became entangled with the problems of loyalty to the church as an institution with influence in the world. St. Augustine (354–430)—the founder of theology, whose influence on Christianity is thought by many to be second only to that of St. Paul—had a great impact on the Middle Ages with his idea of the validity of worldly rule by the church. In *The City of God*, he foresaw the rising of Christianity into an empire on the ruins of Rome. He projected the role of the church as the divine-led ruler over all nations bound by common loyalty to the church.

In this earthly world, Augustine took the position that there is a duty of loyalty to an evil, as well as to a righteous, ruler since "God gives happiness in the kingdom of heaven to the pious alone, but gives kingly power on earth both to the pious and the impious, as it may please Him. . . ." Even the dreaded Nero Caesar, who reached, according to Augustine, the summit of vice and cruelty, ruled by the will of God because "power and domination are not given even to such men save by the providence of the most high God, when he judges that the state of human affairs is worthy of such lords." Tyrants rule as a punishment for sins, and we fulfill God's purpose through loyalty to Him, because behind each act of God there is a "hidden cause, known better to God than to us, depending on the diversity of the merits of the human race." (*St. Augustine's City of God, A Select Library of the Nicene and Post Nicene Fathers of the Christian Church*, Vol. II, ed. Philip Schaff, Wm. Eerdmans, 1979, pp. 101–103.)

The idea of the unity of Christendom and the idea that the world should be turned into an organized Kingdom of Heaven where the underpinnings of the theory that the kings of terrestrial states owe loyalty to the Pope, the high priest and the divine monarch of Christendom. This idea of a divine world dominion ruled by the church, which would bring about the peace of Christ throughout the world, was nourished by the church throughout the Middle Ages. This idea, however, did not appeal to the secular world, and from the fifth through the fifteenth centuries, history records a divergence of views about the role of the church and the consequent failure of the idea of a divine world government.

C. St. Thomas Aquinas

Another principal saint and doctor of the Roman Catholic Church, St. Thomas Aquinas (1225–1274), differs from Augustine by declaring the right to resist tyranny. His monumental contention was that reason and faith cannot deny each other's findings, although they may differ in their procedure. (This idea was opposed to another strand of thought arising in the thirteenth century, represented by the Arab philosopher Averroes and the Franciscan scholastic philosophers Duns Scotus and William of Occam, that truth in faith need not be compatible with reason and that there cannot be a rational demonstration of God's existence and of the immortality of the soul.) Aquinas in the *Summa Theologica* reaches the conclusion—based both on reason and on faith—that "Man is bound to obey secular princes in so far as this is required by the order of justice. Wherefore if the prince's authority is not just but usurped, or if he commands what is unjust, his subjects are not bound to obey him." Aquinas sees no sedition in being disloyal to a tyrant because "indeed it is the tyrant rather that is guilty of sedition since he encourages discord and sedition among his subjects, that he may lord over them more securely; for this is tyranny, being conducive to the private good of the ruler, and to the injury of the multitude."

St. Thomas makes the distinction between loyalty to the office and loyalty to the tyrant occupying the office. He advocates obedience as a "special virtue," but in matters concerning human behavior, "a subject is bound to obey his superior only within the sphere of his authority." Aquinas also makes a clear distinction between the subject's loyalty to God and to his earthly superior. There are some matters in which no earthly master has jurisdiction and in which one owes obedience only to God. Only in matters where the "superior stands between God and his subjects" is the subject bound to obey his superior, whereas "in respect of other matters the subject is immediately under God, by Whom he is taught either by the natural or by written law." (*Summa Theologica*, Vol. III, Christian Classics, 1948.)

The Renaissance—The Divorce of Loyalty from Ethics

The period of transition from medieval to modern times known as the Renaissance, which is generally identified as stretching from the fourteenth through the seventeenth century, is marked by a flowering of creative literature, by the rebirth of classic architecture and the development of cities with distinctive and beautiful buildings, by economic changes brought by the Crusades that had opened the routes to the East, by discoveries and inventions that tended to civilize the life of man, and by the patronage of artists by princes and men of wealth. It was an age of social and intellectual achievement in the field of science, in the exploration of the world, and in the conquest of the seas and of man's ignorance about the mysteries of the sky and the earth. In this age of change, Columbus landed on the shores of the New World, and Europe started to reap the benefits to be derived from the discovery of America.

A. Machiavelli

The Renaissance was the age of a weakening of the hold of the Catholic Church upon the consciences of men and of the concentration of power in the hands of European monarchs, such as the Holy Roman Emperor Charles V (who held sway over more territory than any other European ruler), King

Francis I of France, and King Henry VIII of England. The art of kingcraft suitable for such monarchs was expounded by such political theorists as Niccolo Machiavelli (1469–1527) and Thomas Hobbes (1588–1679). Their powerful minds spread their influence everywhere, and their ideas were received as the quintessence of political wisdom. By divorcing the study of politics from the study of ethics, Machiavelli and Hobbes completely dissevered themselves from the older concepts of the power of conscience in men, as well as from traditional concepts of loyalty.

Machiavelli saw as the core of political success and effectiveness force unrestricted by considerations of generally accepted moral values. In order to achieve political ends, he argued, a ruler may lie, deceive, intrigue, conspire, or use any kind of crooked means. The ruler "must not mind incurring the charge of cruelty for the purpose of keeping the subjects united and faithful." (*The Prince*, The New Library, 1952, p. 89.) The Duke of Gloucester (later Richard III) in Shakespeare's *Henry VI* personifies Machiavelli's ideas calling for complete disregard of moral bonds and responsibilities when he declares:

> "Why, I can smile, and murder whiles I smile;
> And cry content to that which grieves my heart;
> And wet my cheeks with artificial tears,
> And frame my face to all occasions. . . .
> I can add colours to the chameleon;
> Change shapes with Proteus for advantages;
> And set the murderous Machiavel to school.
> Can I do this, and cannot get a crown?"

Born in 1469, Machiavelli witnessed the troubled political life of his native Florence and concluded that the only way for the state to become a dynamic, aggressive entity was to increase the power of the prince. In foreign policy, the prince should seek to defend his less powerful neighbors and to weaken the stronger ones. "A prince should therefore have no other aim or thought, nor take up any other thing for his study, but war and its organization and discipline, for that is the only art that is necessary to one who commands. . . ." (*Ibid.*, pp. 46–47.) (It seems that *The Prince* continues to serve as a handbook for Soviet rulers in their policy toward the satellites in Eastern Europe and toward minorities at home.)

On the domestic front, Machiavelli argued, the policies of the prince should also be divorced from moral values. Since it is difficult for a ruler to be both loved and feared, "it is much safer to be feared than loved." (*Ibid.*, p. 90.) Although it seems advisable for the prince to be merciful, faithful, humane, sincere, and religious, "in order to maintain the state" he should not hesitate "to act against faith, against charity, against humanity, and against religion." (*Ibid.*, p. 93.) Machiavelli suggests that the prince discourage attempts to advise him (unless he asks for such advice), "for men will always be false to you unless they are compelled by necessity to be true." (*Ibid.*, p. 117.) The prince should use hypocrisy, since it is expedient for him to seem to his subjects "all mercy, faith, integrity, humanity and religion." (*Ibid.*, p. 94.)

If, according to Machiavelli, the prince should violate any kind of legal and moral commitments in the interest of self-aggrandisement and absolute power, the question arises, what are the responsibilities of his subjects when the prince abuses his powers? Is there a place for loyalty to the prince who is outside law, integrity, and morality? Although it seems that any kind of evil is condoned within the precepts of Machiavellianism, a closer examination of Machiavelli's writings will reveal his awareness of the importance of traditional moral values, such as loyalty, patriotism, and love. He was keenly aware of the importance of loyalty when he recommended that the prince should have the loyalty of the people, because force is not enough and "it is necessary for a prince to possess the friendship of the people; otherwise he has no resource in times of adversity." (*Ibid.*, p. 65.)

Machiavelli in the *Discourses* also acknowledges that the power of the state must be endowed with lawful authority in order for it to endure. He asked the reader to note

> "how much more praise those Emperors merited who, after Rome became an empire, conformed to the laws like good princes, than those who took the opposite course; and he will see that Titus, Nerva, Trajan, Hadrian, Antoninus, and Marcus Aurelius did not require the Praetorians nor the multitudinous legions to defend them, because they were protected by their own good conduct,

[by] the good will of the people, and by the love of the Senate."

Machiavelli's passionate love for Italy and his recognition of the importance of such virtues as loyalty, mercy, faith, and integrity show that some historians—in spite of the identification of his precepts with everything that is considered to be immoral and inhuman—are justified in hailing him as a leading political philosopher and the founder of modern political science.

B. Hobbes

The whole tenor of Machiavelli's thought about the omnipotent prince was echoed by the English philosopher who exalted absolute monarchy, Thomas Hobbes. The foundation of his ethics is the doctrine of the original nature of man. According to the fundamental law of nature, every man has the right to everything, and when he cannot obtain all that he desires, he "may seek, and use, all helps, and advantages of war." From this law derives the second law, that a man is willing, when others are also, to lay down his selfish rights to create the state, "and he contended with so much liberty against other men, as he would allow other men against himself." (*Leviathan*, Basil Blackwell, 1960, p. 85.)

This surrender of rights and establishment of an absolute sovereignty, Hobbes contends, is a contract made by "every man with every man." This agreement is made by people with each other, not with the sovereign. To obtain peace and secure the common defense, men "confer all their power and strength upon one man, or upon an assembly of men," and by doing so "they may reduce all their wills, by plurality of voices unto one will." In other words, the covenant is made in such a manner as if every man would say to every other man, "I authorize and give up my right of governing myself, to this man, or to this assembly of men, on this condition, that you give up thy right to him, and authorize all his actions in like manner." (*Ibid.*, p. 12.)

In a civil society that is the creation of a covenant between men, peace and security are obtained at the price of replacing freedom by law and rights by obligation. By the voluntary surrender of the natural right of each man to an authority, a new entity, which Hobbes calls an "artificial man," is created, a commonwealth. There are, according to Hobbes, three types of commonwealth—monarchy, aristocracy, and democracy. The sovereignty residing in monarchy is absolutely supreme and outside the restraints of the contract: "There can happen no breach of covenant on the part of the sovereign; and consequently none of his subjects, by any pretense of forfeiture, can be freed from his subjection." (*Ibid.*, p. 114.)

Hobbes makes no distinction between a good and a tyrannical government, "because the name of tyranny signifieth nothing more, nor less than the name of sovereignty, be it in one, or many men, saving that they that use the former word, are understood to be angry with them they call tyrants." (*Ibid.*, p. 463.) Supreme power is indispensable for supreme authority, and only power can perpetually enforce the covenant made by people with each other: "Covenants without the Sword, are but words." Without force and terror the laws of a higher nature, such as justice, modesty, and mercy, could not be enforced since they are contrary to man's natural passions of "pride, revenge, and the like." (*Ibid.*, p. 109.)

Is there a place for loyalty in "this great Leviathan, which is called the State"? Hardly, since loyalty is replaced by total submission of the subject to the ruler. To ensure the order of the commonwealth, there must be obedience to the will of the sovereign. This idea also implies a lack of loyalty to one's country. If a subject becomes a prisoner in war and can save his life by becoming subject to the victor, "he hath the liberty to accept the condition, and having accepted it, is the subject of him that took him." Furthermore, if the monarch subdued by war renders himself to become a subject of the victor, his subjects "become obliged to the victor." (*Ibid.*, p. 145.) There is no personal loyalty to the monarch; whoever conquers and provides security and peace ought to be obeyed.

The Dominant Role of the People

It is not surprising that the immoral tendencies of Hobbes' doctrines aroused a storm of abuse as well as serious criticism. He was denounced for being an apostle of despotism, for holding religion in contempt, and for teaching, as one of his critics expressed it, "one of the meanest of all ethical theories." The most important antagonists of Hobbes' concept of a contract of submission were

John Locke, who assigned in the contractual relation a dominant role to the people and a subservient role to the government, and Jean-Jacques Rousseau, who completely rejected the concept of the contract of government.

A. John Locke

John Locke (1632–1704), called the "founder of British empiricism," saw the justification of government in the consent of the governed, based on the natural rights of the people. He differentiated the origins of a society from the establishment of the government. Refuting the Hobbesian thesis of the anarchistic and savage state of nature before the establishment of government, Locke maintained that men in the state of nature were free, equal, and independent and that no one could be "put out of this estate and subjected to the political power of another without his own consent." (*Two Treatises of Government*, ed. Thomas T. Cook, Hofner Publishing Company, 1947, p. 168.) The law of the state of nature is reason, which commands that no one should injure another's freedom, life, or property. In remitting power to the majority, men enter society by their own consent. The law established by a majority vote is the only effective method of arriving at decisions in a society aimed at common good.

In support of his theory that the governments of the world were begun in peace and by the consent of the people, Locke lists examples of history. One place he found evidence was in the writings of Jose de Orcosta, a Spanish Jesuit and a missionary to Peru, who in his *Historia Natural y Moral de las Indias* reported that many parts of America had neither kings nor commonwealth, but as the occasion demanded it, they chose their "captains as they please." Locke also frequently quoted the history of Israel. An example is his reference to the passage in the Book of Judges where the Gileadites ask Jephthah to assist them against the Ammonites, "and the people made him head and captain over them." (Judges 11:2.)

The actual use of an agreement between individuals to compose a society is found in the declaration made by the Pilgrim Fathers on the *Mayflower* in 1620, in which occurs the phrase, "We do solemnly and mutually, in the presence of God and of one another, covenant and combine ourselves together into a civil body politic." The natural implication of such an agreement is that the government, as a servant of society, is bound by the provisions by which it had been established and by the will of a free people.

Although the state of nature was governed by law, according to Locke, disputes arose among men engaged in the pursuit of their individual rights. The purpose of political society was to overcome the lack of an authority to judge the controversies between the parties engaged in disputes. The state thus became a judicial body interpreting the law of nature for individuals. This does not mean at all that the state can deprive these individuals of their natural rights. Through the social contract, the individual preserves his natural rights, giving up only the part necessary for the community to live effectively. This arrangement between people and their rulers differentiates the loyalty of the people from the loyalty of the rulers.

The loyalty of individuals consists of reverence for law and respect for authority. Since the people are dominant and the government is subservient, the loyalty of a ruler consists not only in adhering to the laws that bind his power but also in making the well-being of the public the end purpose of his government. Consequently, whosoever in authority exceeds the power given him by the law and makes improper use of the force he has under his command, "may be opposed as any other man who by force invades the right of another." (*Two Treatises of Government*, p. 224.)

People owe no loyalty to those who commit a breach of trust, subvert the government, and poison "the fountain of public security." Locke—who witnessed the civil war and the "Glorious Revolution" (which deposed King James II, according to the resolution passed by the 1688 Convention parliament)—justifies the revolt of the British people against tyranny, thus setting a precedent for the justification of the American Revolution. According to a similar argument, the contract by which the American colonists promised allegiance to the British crown was broken by George III. It was their right to resist his illegal use of authority and to redirect political power into avenues reflecting the will of the people.

B. Common Loyalty to a Just Purpose

Locke's concept of a society based on a "compact" (which we would call a "constitution"), which covers the terms of the people's agreement to form a society, and on "trust," the fiduciary relation that determines the limits of the government's power, was adopted by Thomas Paine, the brilliant Englishman whose pamphlet entitled *Common Sense* had an enormous effect on American colonists. His appeal, "The blood of the slain, the weeping voice of nature cries, 'Tis time to part,' " convinced thousands of colonists of the necessity to separate from England. In his *The Rights of Man*, Thomas Paine assigned to the people the role of a superior partner in their relations with the government. The people have natural rights, according to Paine, while the government has mainly an obligation to be the servant of society.

The impact of the powerful teaching of Locke on the framers of our Constitution is not limited to the justification of the right of resistance to unjust and unlawful force. His concept of natural rights became a universal claim of mankind. Declarations marked by ideas of natural rights guaranteeing that citizens would not be abused by the government preface the Declaration of Independence and the constitutions adopted between 1776 and 1783 by Maryland, Massachusetts, New Hampshire, South Carolina, Vermont, and Virginia. The universalism of the natural law idea also marks the French Declaration of the Rights of Man and of the Citizen (1789), which proclaimed that the purpose of every political association is "the preservation of the natural and imprescriptible rights of man," which include the right to resist oppression.

It should be noted that our Declaration of Independence with its indictment of the King of

England did not see in the rights of Americans as a nationality the reason for forming a new state. Rather, it justified the founding of our nation on the need to protect the fundamental human rights to life, liberty, and the pursuit of happiness that had been violated by the king. The United States was unique, at the time of its founding, in that its cohesiveness was based not simply on geographical, racial, or linguistic ties but rather on an allegiance to the conception of natural rights which are beyond the reach of any government and which transcend geographical boundaries.

The Constitution should always be read in the spirit of this loyalty, which is not to a king or to a piece of territory but to a purpose, namely that of protecting citizens against the exercise of arbitrary and capricious power by the government. As an outstanding exponent of the political philosophy of American history, Hans J. Morgenthau, expressed it:

> "A nation which was built upon a common loyalty to a certain purpose, whose citizens have come together voluntarily to share in the achievement of that purpose, which owes its very existence to a revolt against arbitrary impediments to the achievement of that purpose—such a nation stands or falls, as a nation, with its loyalty to that purpose." (*The Purpose of American Politics,* Vintage Books, 1960, p. 56.)

In support of the "self-evident truth" that all men are endowed with certain unalienable rights, that the governments derive their just powers from the consent of the governed, and that it is the right of the people to abolish a government that "becomes destructive of these ends," the representatives of the twelve states that agreed to the text of the Declaration pledged to each other "our lives, our fortunes and our sacred honor." They found a goal, an "American purpose" to which they pledged their common loyalty "with a firm reliance on the protection of divine Providence."

The Constitution and the American political system are the living manifestation of the silent compact between citizens and their government to cooperate in the achievement of this purpose. Such a purpose—to which we are referring in our definition of loyalty as a "just purpose"—makes moral demands on our attitudes and actions. These demands have been met in some of our national achievements, but they have also been answered with denials and by sporadic violations of that purpose. The failures can be explained by the fact that, in the search for the substance of the "common" and "just" purpose we seek, we are confronted with a conflict of views, some of them too narrow and others too exhaustive. These diverse views range from single-minded, exclusive loyalty to a leader or movement to a pluralistic loyalty resulting from the interaction of coexisting and competing loyalties to religious, economic, natural, or racial groups.

Multiple and Competing Loyalties

Single loyalty provides no safer path to the achievement of the purpose of equality in freedom through a common loyalty (the ideal to which our forefathers pledged themselves) than pluralistic loyalty does. History gives us numerous examples of followers of a leader or of a movement who have been browbeaten into rejecting their religious and political beliefs and their families and into betraying their friends in order to make them utterly devoted to their leader and his movement. Hitler demanded and received absolute loyalty, and Khoumeni is regarded as a fountain of wisdom by his followers.

In the case of multiple loyalties, the common loyalty is endangered when one of the competing loyalties is raised above this loyalty to the "certain purpose" which the founders of this country agreed to achieve. This purpose can be achieved only when the spirit of reconciliation, not of hate, is at the heart of the multiple loyalties to labor unions, industrial organizations, and national, racial, or religious groups. This purpose can be achieved when behind each loyalty lies an understanding of the law of sowing and reaping, when a law of service and sacrifice underlies its existence.

Some denials of the American purpose should be attributed to the fact that a distinction should be drawn between the moral and social behavior of individuals and of racial, national, and economic groups. Human societies and social groups have less capacity than individual men and women to comprehend the needs of others and less ability to consider interests other than their own. As Reinhold

Niebuhr pointed out, a human group has less ability to comprehend the needs of others and more unrestrained egoism than the individuals who compose the group. Individuals are capable, on occasion, of preferring the advantages of others to their own, and their sentiments of sympathy and sense of justice can lead them in the direction of altruism. The morality of groups is, however, inferior to that of individuals. Man's collective behavior, because of collective egoism, "can never be brought completely under the dominion of reason or conscience." (*Moral Man and Immoral Society*, Charles Scribner's Sons, 1960, p. xii.) The truths proclaimed as "self-evident" by our forefathers appeared meaningless and not "self-evident" at all to some of the political groups that shaped the history of our nation.

One example of the discrepancy between private and public morality looms large in the history of our country. In the words of Lincoln, the Declaration of Independence "gave promise that in due time the weights should be lifted from the shoulders of all men" in the world. Jefferson warned that our "falling into anarchy would decide forever the destinies of mankind, and seal the political heresy that man is incapable of self-government" since we are "the only depositories of the sacred fire of liberty." And, yet, the framers of the Constitution compromised the principle of equality—which had been enshrined so nobly in the Declaration of Independence in the famous phrase "all men are created equal"—with its antithesis, slavery.

Multiple loyalties can create tensions, but competing loyalties should not debilitate the spirit of common purpose that should characterize our nation, since the denial of this purpose will alienate the people from America itself. The thoughts of the French statesman Turgot, expressed in a letter of March 22, 1778, concerning Americans and their new republican government, reflect the sentiment shared today by oppressed countries:

> "They are the hope of the human race. They should be the model. They must prove to the world, as a fact, that men can be both free and peaceful and can dispense with the trammels of all sorts which tyrants and charlatans of every costume have presumed to impose under the pretext of public safety. They must give the example of political liberty, of religious liberty, of commercial and industrial liberty. The asylum which America affords to the oppressed of all nations will console the world."

A common loyalty faces the danger of failure to obtain a general consensus because we try to find legitimacy in pluralistic loyalties to all aspects of society's life, including our relations to the church, to the state, and to various economic, political, racial, and national groups. Among the tensions caused by multiple loyalties, the freedoms of religion, of speech, and of association have been at the heart of the so-called loyalty controversies that have occurred throughout our history. Broadly speaking, common loyalty to the American purpose embodies a standard of devotion to our country that satisfies a sense of fairness and good citizenship. It is not imprisoned within the limits of any rigid formula or within a fixed content of the meaning of good citizenship. If common loyalty demands commitment to the well-being of our country, it should be expected that earnest citizens can hold contrary views and that such differences in opinion should in no way reflect on their common loyalty to the "American purpose." The discussion of some of these "loyalty controversies" may deepen our understanding of the meaning of common loyalty.

Conflicting Loyalties

A. Church and State

The history of the early Middle Ages is in large part the history of the struggle between the Popes in Rome and the emperors of Western Europe. The claims for power of the secular rulers were opposed by the Popes, who insisted upon their right to absolute rule of all Christendom and the supremacy of the church over emperors, kings, and princes. Papal Rome saw world dominion through the establishment of a religious government of mankind with its center in Rome as the only way to obtain the "peace of Christ throughout the world." These controversies between the secular rulers and Rome existed for centuries, whether in a suppressed state or in outward conflict.

The question of investiture, for instance—the

argument whether the emperor or the Pope should appoint bishops—was one of the most serious controversies, since in many kingdoms the church had vast properties, levied taxes, and had its own law courts, with Rome serving as the highest court of appeals. Since the church had become a state within a state, with powers reaching far beyond spiritual functions, the matter of who had the decisive voice in appointing bishops who controlled large domains became a vital question.

Saint Augustine's idea of the world as a "spiritual society of the predestined faithful" developed into a political policy advocating the divinely led ruling power of the church over all nations. The City of God advocated by Augustine, however, was not satisfied with its role of enhancing the spiritual values preached by Jesus of Nazareth; it wanted to dominate the world.

B. The City of God and the City of Man

One purpose of the Crusades was to extend the influence of Rome, the Latin church, over the territories now known as the Middle East and to undermine the Eastern Empire with the emperor of Constantinople dominant in the Greek-speaking Orthodox church. One of the most important examples of outward, violent public conflict took place in the time of the Emperor Frederick II, who was twice excommunicated by Pope Gregory IX for failing to start on his promised crusade. Frederick II, in turn, denounced the corruption in the church and urged all the princes in Europe to confiscate church property.

When biblical beliefs flow into political life, the result is acknowledgment and respect for human rights, religious tolerance, and freedom of the individual conscience. The Reformation and the Enlightenment were revolts against theocratic, dogmatic ecclesiastical institutions and not against traditional biblical values. Martin Luther was a Catholic when he protested against ecclesiastical imperialism. The Protestants—using this term to apply to all those who dissented from the mother church—set themselves against complete allegiance to the priest, bishop, and Pope and not against allegiance to the Bible, which they accepted as the absolute norm and the sole arbitrator of religious doctrines. Opposition between the political and spiritual realms disappears when the two cities rest on a common foundation, the legacy of the Christian belief in the dignity and worth of every individual.

The religious influences on those who framed and adopted the Constitution cannot be denied. Among the framers of the Constitution were nineteen Episcopalians, eight Congregationalists, seven Presbyterians, two Roman Catholics, two Quakers, one Methodist, and one member of the Dutch Reformed Church. They represented a cross section of the American religious bodies of that day. Throughout the history of the United States there have always been reasonable accommodations between the church and state, such as tax exemptions for property used for religious purposes, tax deductibility of contributions to churches, and military chaplaincies.

The aggregate of the "self-evident truths"

expressed in the Declaration of Independence and later in the Bill of Rights reflects the belief of the builders of the republic that only people with a moral purpose can be free and that freedom can survive if the people, beyond the purpose of mere survival, are governed by moral law, which has its roots in religion. The separation of church and state by the Founding Fathers of the Land of the Free did not imply that religion was considered merely as a private affair. On the contrary, religion has had a striking impact on the forming of our nation. In a nation "under God," which recognizes the dignity and worth of every human being, God is best honored by free men with liberty of conscience. In a free society, the government must, therefore, assert freedom of conscience as an indefeasible right of the individual, who is not accountable to the government or to others for his religious beliefs.

The conviction, held by the great men who have led our country, that freedom has its roots in a belief in divine ordinance is demonstrated in many of the most famous American documents. The writers of the Declaration of Independence proclaimed the birth of our nation "with a firm reliance on the protection of Divine Providence." George Washington began his inaugural address with "fervent supplication to that Almighty Being who rules over the Universe" and in his farewell address besought "the Almighty to avert or mitigate" whatever evils the new republic might face. Abraham Lincoln prayed at Gettysburg "that this nation, under God, shall have a new birth of freedom."

The religious atmosphere in this country, in the

words of Alexis de Tocqueville, "was the first thing that struck him" on his arrival in the United States. In his desire to understand the reason for this phenomenon, he questioned "the faithful of all communions." He particularly sought the society of clergymen, who "are depositories of the various creeds and have a personal interest in their survival." His research convinced him that the "main reason for the quiet sway of religion over their country was the complete separation of church and state." "I have," he wrote, "no hesitation in stating that throughout my stay in America I met nobody, lay or cleric, who did not agree about that." (*Democracy in America*, trans. by George Lawrence, Harper & Row Publishers, 1966, pp. 271–272.)

C. Separation between Church and State

Since religious and spiritual values are interconnected with our political life, the questions arise: What is the meaning of the rule of law that builds "a wall of separation" between church and state? What is the relationship between our loyalties to the state and our loyalties to the church?

The first question on the constitutional guarantee of separation of church and state has been addressed extensively by the Supreme Court. The conclusions it has reached can be enumerated as follows:

Neither state nor federal government can set up a church, nor make laws respecting an establishment of religion or prohibiting the free exercise thereof. Nor can any official, "high or petty," prescribe what shall be orthodox in religion or other matters of opinion or force citizens "to confer by word or act their faith therein."

Neither state nor federal government can pass laws that aid one religion, aid all religions, or prefer one religion over another.

Neither state nor federal government can, openly or secretly, participate in the affairs of any religious organizations or groups and vice versa.

No tax in any amount, large or small, can be levied to support any religious activities or institutions, whatever they may be called or whatever form they may adopt to teach or practice religion.

Do these conclusions call for ignoring the traditional, biblical moral values in making political decisions? Not at all, unless we wish to eliminate the distinction between good and evil and convert our political system into a barbaric tyranny that robs individuals of their freedom and human rights. In making political decisions, we must, however, realize that in a world with tyrannical regimes armed with nuclear power it would be unfeasible to base political decisions solely on moral principles. As a matter of expediency and of mankind's survival, we must deal with totalitarian governments, but we should never disregard the reality of having nations enslaved in a large part of the world. In the international game of political power, the voices against the immorality of apartheid should be joined by voices against the atrocities committed by communist

regimes. Under no circumstances should moral considerations be eliminated in assessing our political
goals.

To answer the second question concerning our
loyalties to the state and to the church, it should be
noted that on the domestic scene some of the furor
caused by the Supreme Court's interpretation of the
rule of the separation of church and state has reached
almost the stage of obsession. Permission for saying
a school prayer, for instance, was attacked as
vigorously as if granting that permission amounted
to turning this country into a theocracy in Khoumeni's style. The so-called fundamentalists defend organized prayer during the school day with as much
vigor as if allowing the prayer amounted to a remedy against the drug culture, the growth of crime, out-
of-wedlock pregnancy, and the other highly disturbing trends in our society.

The interpretation that should be followed is sovereign reverence to the intentions of the framers of our
Constitution, who did not expect the state to behave
as if it were a church or the church to behave as if
it were a state. James Madison, author of the First
Amendment, wrote:

> ". . . [I]t is proper to take alarm at the first experi-
> ment on our liberties. Who does not see that the
> same authority which can establish Christianity,
> in exclusion of all other religions, may establish
> with the same ease any particular sect of
> Christians, in exclusion of all other sects? That
> the same authority which can force a citizen to
> contribute three pence only of his property for

the support of any one establishment, may force
him to conform to any other establishment in all
cases whatsoever?"

The position of "neutrality" advocated by some is
not the solution to the existing controversies. Our
Constitution is not neutral in matters concerning
basic values since freedom of religion and of conscience is an explicit postulate demanding active
interaction and not passive neutrality. Neutrality can
be applied only toward differences in the interpretation of ideas and practices by churches of various
denominations as to what is permitted by the Scriptures and toward differences in catechisms, creeds,
symbols, and confessional standards developed by
the practices and beliefs of various churches. These
differences cannot be settled by the coercive rule of
secular law and must be left to the free conscience
of each individual.

The presidential election of 1960 brought into
clearer focus than any event before or since the issue
of loyalty to the church and of loyalty to the state in
American political life. In the history of this country,
John F. Kennedy was only the second Roman
Catholic to be nominated for the presidency. At the
time of his nomination, there was a heated controversy about the capability of a Catholic President
to preserve his independence from the hierarchy in
performing his duties.

The most notable instance of Kennedy's desire to
address this issue was the famous meeting with the
Greater Houston Ministerial Association on
September 12, 1960. Kennedy made an opening

statement and accepted questions from the floor from the Protestant ministers gathered. His stand on the issue was forthright:

> "I believe in an America where the separation of church and state is absolute—where no Catholic prelate would tell the President (should he be a Catholic) how to act and no Protestant minister would tell his parishioners for whom to vote— where no church or church school is granted any public funds or political preference—and where no man is denied public office merely because his religion differs from the President who might appoint him or the people who might elect him.
>
> "I believe in an America that is officially neither Catholic, Protestant, nor Jewish—where no public official either requests or accepts instructions on public policy from the Pope, the National Council of Churches or any other ecclesiastical source—where no religious body seeks to impose its will directly or indirectly upon the general populace or the public acts of its officials—and where religious liberty is so indivisible that an act against one church is treated as an act against all." (Theodore H. White, *The Making of the President 1960*, Atheneum Publishers, 1961, Appendix C, p. 391.)

Kennedy apparently convinced enough voters of his independence from clerical dictate that he received from Protestants more than half of the votes that elected him. (*Ibid.*, p. 357.)

Churches have always been involved in public

policy and have always addressed the moral aspects of political issues. The abolitionist movement, prohibition, women's suffrage, the conservation of natural resources, the control of monopolies, and public education are all causes which have concerned many groups of mainline Protestants since the birth of our nation. In the early 1960s, the social activism of the churches played a major role in the passage of national civil rights legislation. In recent times the broadening agendas of churches' involvement include positions on abortion, homosexuality, pornography, the feminist movement, teaching of evolution and creationism, and even preoccupation with foreign affairs. Religious forces and values derived from religion have been the essential foundation for our form of government and among the important formative influences on our conduct.

The voice of the churches on issues with major moral content has penetrated various areas of public and private life. As believers in free enterprise, we have come to the realization that the completely uncontrolled process of a "free" economy may cause massive human sufferings when the idea of "free" enterprise becomes an absolute dogma. Compassion for the poor thus became a mark of our nation's tradition, and poverty became ethically intolerable. Unemployment insurance, Social Security, anti-poverty measures, Medicare, and housing bills evidence the acceptance of the government's—as well as society's—responsibility for the poor and for the sick, a responsibility based on moral values nurtured by the churches.

On the international stage, an increased spiritual

involvement on the part of church leaders in political life is evident. Catholic bishops of the Philippines condemned the fraud in the 1986 election and called on the Filipino people to vote their consciences despite intimidation and bribes and to rectify elections described as "unparalleled in the fraudulence of their conduct." After the February 7 elections, the pastoral letter of the Catholic bishops of the Philippines of February 14, 1986, declared that "a government that assumes or retains power through fraudulent means has no moral basis."

Cardinal Jaime Sin, the so-called father of the Philippine revolution, urged the people to show "solidarity" and "support" for the opposition in its attempt to unseat President Ferdinand Marcos. He took an active role in the events leading up to Marcos' fleeing the country. Sin urged Filipinos to form a protective wall around military leaders who had defected from Marcos' army.

Some Catholic circles in the Philippines dissented from the bishops' statement that declared the illegitimacy of the government and called for its overthrow, objecting to this statement as a dangerous step which invaded the political realm and violated the principle of the separation of church and state. The churchmen who joined Cardinal Sin in endorsing the bishops' pastoral letter of February 14 took the position that the church cannot be impartial in matters of morality and honesty, and silence would mean sanctioning the evils of cheating and harassment witnessed during the election. Politics is a human activity, and when people are in danger of being harmed, they maintained, the church has the obligation to speak on behalf of the sanctity of the ballot and to see that human rights are protected.

Moral judgments on a government made by the church are becoming ever more widespread. In Poland we witnessed a moral alliance of the opposition movement known as Solidarity and of the Catholic Church. Solidarity was born in 1979 as a consequence of Pope John Paul II's visit to Poland, described as "Poland's second baptism." It restored the dignity of the people oppressed by the communist regime, and the changed spirit of the Poles gave birth to a movement defending the rights of the worker and upholding fundamental social and moral principles.

Solidarity's policies of openness and nonviolence gained strong support from the Catholic Church. Although it was not one of Solidarity's goals to overthrow the government, Moscow could not tolerate the existence of such a movement enjoying overwhelming national support and the wide participation of the working class. Since Solidarity's dedication to liberty could have ignited the sparks of independence, it was banned by the Polish communist government. The "state of war" declared by the government against Solidarity was followed by mass arrests and imprisonment. The victims of this "war" were Solidarity's leaders—among them Catholic priests who participated in the movement opposed to the totalitarian rule of the Polish version of the Soviet regime.

In Nicaragua, Cardinal Miguel Olando y Bravo strongly opposed the Somoza dictatorship and denounced its crimes and abuses. He played a significant spiritual role in the Sandinista revolution but did not hesitate to denounce the communist government of Nicaragua that grasped power after the revolution for the destruction of the goals of the revolution and of the foundations on which democracy rests. He rejected the legitimacy of the communist government and accused it of mixing and confusing the concepts of faith, the church, the revolution, *Sandinisma*, and the fatherland. The Cardinal's position was challenged and subverted by a group of priests who joined the communist government. Some even became members of the cabinet in defiance of the Pope and the Vatican hierarchy.

This fusion of religion and active participation in politics, especially the holding of elective offices by priests, has been condemned by the Vatican, which saw in such office holding both a conflict in what priests should represent to the faithful and a weakening of this mission caused by their belonging to one party over another. The so-called liberation theology—which asserts that the church should engage in a political struggle for social change—was rejected by Pope John Paul II and other Vatican leaders who believe that the priests should not be involved in direct political action in order to help the poor.

In his concern with the grave questions of social justice and equity in personal, national, and international relations, John Paul II expects the church to play a specific and important role which cannot be identified with nor replaced by the aim of politicians, sociologists, or business or union leaders. The priests who go beyond their role in speaking out on human justice, poverty, hunger, and alienation and take direct political action are not following the directions of Rome.

In Latin America, where nearly half of the world's Catholics live in widespread poverty and most contend with frequent guerrilla wars, the Vatican's views seem irrelevant to priests who are found on the front line of violent social struggle. The vast Latin American movement which is subsumed under the epithet "liberation theology" has therefore arisen and has been condemned by the Vatican for its deformation of theological principles and its disloyalty to the church and to the Pope, who in 1870 was declared by the First Vatican Council to be "endowed with that infallibility which according to the will of the Redeemer, is vouchsafed to the Church when she desires to fix a doctrine of faith or morality." On the televised visit of Pope John Paul II in Nicaragua, the Minister of Culture, Father Ernesto Cardinal, appeared on the screen kneeling before the Pope for a blessing. The Pope, wagging a finger of reproach, sternly reminded him that he must straighten out (*arreglar*) his relations with the Vatican.

In the United States, because of the opposition of the Vatican to having priests in elective office, Rev. Robert Drinan, a Massachusetts congressman—in order to comply with the order issued by Vatican officials to all priests throughout the world to cease secular political activism—in 1980 decided to withdraw from his congressional race to the great disappointment of his friends, aides, and some of the voters in Brookline, Massachusetts. For the same reasons, the Rev. Robert J. Cornell, who was attempting to regain the U.S. House seat from Wisconsin's

Eighth District, gave up his candidacy for Congress as a result of Pope John Paul II's desire to enforce church law that discourages partisan political activity by clergy.

The holding of elective office by clergymen is not a new issue. Alexis de Tocqueville in his *Democracy in America*, the greatest book ever written by a foreigner about America, was surprised to discover that priests and ministers held no public appointments in this country in the early nineteenth century. There was not a single one in the administration, and they were not even represented in the assemblies. As to the attitudes of the clergy, he found that "most of them seemed voluntarily to steer clear of power and to take a sort of professional pride in claiming that it was no concern of theirs." (Tocqueville, p. 272.)

Tocqueville pointed out that this resistance to governmental service by clergymen was not solely voluntary or customary. The constitutions of such states as New York, Virginia, North and South Carolina, Kentucky, Tennessee, and Louisiana specifically prohibited the holding of office by clergymen during the time in which Tocqueville wrote. Article VII, Section 4, of the Constitution of New York of 1821 provided:

"And whereas the ministers of the gospel are, by their profession, dedicated to the service of God and the cure of souls and ought not to be diverted from the great duties of their functions, therefore, no minister of the gospel or priest of any denomination whatever . . . be eligible to or capable of holding any civil or military office or place within this state."

Tocqueville's observations about mingling religion with politics are pertinent to our times. Man, he wrote, shows a natural disgust for existence and an immense longing to exist; he fears annihilation and at the same time scorns life. "These different instincts constantly drive his soul toward contemplation of the next world, and it is religion that leads him thither. Religion, therefore, is only one particular form of hope, and it is as natural to the human heart as hope itself . . . ; faith is the permanent state of mankind."

Having described religion as one of the constituent principles of human nature, Tocqueville reaches the following conclusion:

> "When a religion seeks to found its sway only on the longing for immortality equally tormenting every human heart, it can aspire to universality; but when it comes to uniting itself with a government, it must adopt maxims which apply only to certain nations. Therefore, by allying itself with any political power, religion increases its strength over some but forfeits the hope of reigning overall.
>
> "As long as a religion relies only upon the sentiments which are the consolation of every affliction, it can draw the heart of mankind to itself. When it is mingled with the bitter passions of this world, it is sometimes constrained to defend allies who are such from interest rather than from love; and it has to repulse as adversaries men who still love religion, although they are fighting against religion's allies. Hence religion cannot share

the material strength of the rulers without being burdened with some of the animosity roused against them." (*Ibid.*, p. 273.)

Tocqueville's conclusions recall those that Edmund Burke expressed in 1790 in his famous *Reflections on the French Revolution*. Burke's essay grew out of his response to a sermon preached by a Unitarian minister, Dr. Richard Price, who had praised the Revolution from the pulpit. Burke's remarks are a classic summation of the dangers of fusing religion with politics and of the problem of loyalty to the church versus loyalty to a political cause:

". . . [P]olitics and the pulpit are terms that have little agreement. No sound ought to be heard in the church but the healing voice of Christian charity. The cause of civil liberty and civil government gains as little as that of religion by this confusion of duties. Those who quit their proper character, to assume what does not belong to them, are for the greater part, ignorant both of the character they leave, and of the character they assume. Wholly unacquainted with the world in which they are so fond of meddling, and inexperienced in all its affairs, on which they pronounce with so much passion, they have nothing of politics but the passions they excite. Surely the church is a place where one day's truce ought to be allowed to the dissensions and animosities of mankind." (*Reflections on the French Revolution*, P. F. Collier & Son, 1909, p. 160.)

Since free institutions derive much of their moral vitality from religion, it is the responsibility of the church to enter the public arena to nurture the broad moral values on which the foundation of our democracy rests. The chief mission of the church is to develop the individual's religious conscience; an attempt to advise him on the adequacy of machinery to be used in domestic or international relations will only hinder the role of the church. It is not the responsibility of the church to endorse legislation or policies which involve technical elements that call for special knowledge and experience.

It is outside the intellectual and moral competence of the clergy to advise parishioners whether they should buy gold krugerrands or push United States investments in South Africa, as a Protestant minister suggested upon his return from that country. It is outside the objective of ethical concern to recommend changes in lending policies of the World Bank and the International Monetary Fund, as did the 1986 pastoral letter of the National Conference of Catholic Bishops called "Economic Justice for All." The church may promote free education in order to provide all youth with the right to equal opportunities to develop their capabilities. No one expects, however, that the church is well equipped to suggest what kind of state or federal offices should be engaged in extending aid to education.

Old age and ill health have always been of genuine concern to the church, but is it the responsibility of the church to act as an arbiter on the organization of Medicare or of Social Security, which involves technical elements that call for special knowledge and experience? Freedom of association calls for the right to organize labor unions, but the authority of the church is undermined when it calls either for support or for repeal of the "right to work" laws. This caution should also apply to international relations, where it is necessary to deal with existing realities and practical measures which do not always fulfill the church's visions of and aspirations for justice.

The relationship of the City of God to the City of Man can be compared with the use of a compass in navigation. A compass points the way to a destination but is not expected to solve practical problems of navigation. Similarly, the church is admirably fitted to pointing toward the ends society should strive for but should not be expected to identify the technical means, an act demanding training and experience, by which those ends should be reached. The noble ends of spiritual life are often difficult to harmonize with the reality of domestic problems and international relations. At home we accept only with a certain suspicion—whether justified or not—the assurances of moral motives and spiritual purpose from those who are professionally active in political life. On the international stage, if the City of Man unreservedly adopts the lofty principles embodied in the Sermon on the Mount, it may find itself defenseless against the evils posed by the forces of totalitarianism with its military machines aimed at the destruction of the Free World.

There is always the peril of brutalizing the City of God by associating it with the game of politics in the City of Man. The City of God loses its spiritual purity when it associates itself with man-made dogmas and

the means used in the City of Man to succeed in practical politics. Had the Church allowed itself to
become the champion of changing political or economic theories, it would have suffered the fate of
these passing dogmas. Calvin's idea of social reconstruction through the iron supervision of the
omnipotent church—which would include control of
markets, crafts, rents, interest, prices, and all other
economic activities—was later decried as tyranny of
the clergy. In Iran the emergence of a theocratic
social order is marked with a brutality characteristic only of totalitarian regimes that reject religion as
an operative part of social ideas. The two cities
should be kept apart.

Loyalty and Academic Freedom

The widespread student unrest which we witnessed
in the late 1960s and early 1970s—which was
encouraged in many quarters by members of institutional faculties—spawned renewed discussion about
the compatibility of loyalty to our nation with academic freedom. Can these two values, each essential
to democracy, be preserved without sacrificing
loyalty in the interest of academic freedom or
without imposing any straitjacket on the intellectual
leaders in our colleges and universities in the interest
of loyalty? This question is not characteristic only of
the times of the campus disorders; it was also discussed in the early days of our nation. When on
March 4, 1825, the first classes met at the new University of Virginia, Jefferson's resolution on the
"principles which are to be taught" was condemned

by some of his critics as an imposition of a partisan yoke of loyalty on the educational life of the University.

Jefferson, the rector of the new school, offered in his resolution a list of six books or documents underlying, in the opinion of the Board of Visitors, principles of government which should be "inculcated" and that are "generally approved by our fellow citizens." John Locke's *Essay concerning the true original extent and end of civil government* and Algernon Sidney's *Discourses on Government* were recommended for their treatment of "the general principles of liberty and the rights of man in nature and in society." The "best guides" to the "distinctive principles of the government" were to be found in the remaining four: (1) the Declaration of Independence, as "the fundamental act of union" of the United States; (2) the book known by the title of *The Federalist*, "being an authority to which appeal is habitually made by all, and rarely declined or denied by any as evidence of the general opinion of those who framed, and of those who accepted the Constitution of the U.S. on questions as to its genuine meaning"; (3) the Resolution of the General Assembly of Virginia in 1799, on the subject of the Alien and Sedition Laws, "which appeared in accord with the predominant sense of the people of the U.S."; and (4) the valedictory address of President Washington, "as conveying political lessons of peculiar value."

The preamble of the resolution declared that it is the duty of the University's board to provide that none of the principles of government "be inculcated which are incompatible with those on which the

Constitution of this state and of the U.S. were genuinely based, in the common opinion." For this reason the board found it necessary to point out the sources where the principles of government "are to be found legitimately developed." The books and documents suggested by the resolution, except for the Virginia Resolutions of 1798–1799 drafted by Jefferson and Madison, hardly present partisan political philosophies. Alexander Hamilton, who bitterly opposed Jefferson and was openly antagonistic to his interpretation of the Constitution, was one of the main contributors to *The Federalist.* However, the preamble's provision that forbade teaching principles that are unreconcilable with those on which the Constitution's are based, "in the common opinion," was capable of encroaching upon the freedom of communication of ideas, particularly in the academic environment.

The concept of "common opinion" tends to impinge upon the sensitive area of freedom of inquiry. As the U.S. Supreme Court pointed out, "No field of education is so thoroughly comprehended by man that new discoveries cannot yet be made. Particularly is that true in the social sciences, where few, if any, principles are accepted as absolutes.... Teachers and students must always remain free to inquire, to study and to evaluate, to gain new maturity and understanding; otherwise our civilization will stagnate and die." (*Sweezy v. State of New Hampshire,* 354 U.S. 234, 250, 77 S. Ct. 1203, 1211–1212 [1957].)

Academic freedom is indispensable to a democratic society. It gives vitality to the process of learning and teaching. Unorthodoxy or dissent may be in the vanguard of democratic thought, and the absence of such voices may be a symptom of grave apathy in our society. Does this mean that academic freedom permits disregard for certain established moral standards in the processes of inquiry and thought? Not at all. It is subject to conditions which maintain the essential purpose of a university, which is to seek the truth.

A qualified person who seeks to fulfill the mission of a university by searching for truth has the right to teach conclusions that seem to him reasonably valid in the light of objective scholarship and intellectual integrity. This academic freedom carries with it duties correlative with rights. The 1940 Basic Statement on Academic Freedom of the American Association of University Professors states, "The teacher is entitled to freedom in the classroom in discussing his subject but should be careful not to introduce into his teaching controversial matter which has no relation to his subject." In 1956, the AAUP asserted, "The academic community has a duty to defend society and itself from subversion of the educational process by dishonest tactics, including political conspiracies to deceive students and lead them into acceptance of dogmas or false causes."

Academic freedom is not a citizen's birthright. It is a right that must be earned and can be enjoyed only by those who meet standards of qualification that are an indispensable condition of professional performance. Academic freedom is granted only to scholars truly seeking to reach the truth by applying objective scholarship, not to propagandists who try to dictate their political views and use the classrooms for political purposes. As long as academic freedom is not used to subvert the educational process "by dishonest tactics, including political conspiracies" leading to the acceptance of poisonous and false dogmas, there is no conflict between academic freedom and loyalty to the nation.

In a democractic society there will always be controversial issues, but the focus of both loyalty and academic freedom is the same; search for the truth and progress of society through the progress of knowledge. The focus of both is the pursuit of truth and originality and the acceptance of duties and responsibilities as a correlative to the right of academic freedom and to the rights of citizenship. Loyalty and academic freedom call for commitment to preserving our cultural values and to nurturing the means for responsible reform of social institutions based upon established standards of moral judgment.

Loyalty—An Essential Virtue in a Democracy

In my book *Three Sources of National Strength*, patriotism was identified as one of those sources. Loyalty to the nation was listed as one of the virtues distinctive to patriotism, since it means the fidelity that emanates from a love of and devotion to one's country. The most important aspects involved in loyalty to the nation and to the government discussed in that book are pertinent to my arguments concerning the role of loyalty in the cultivation of democracy and in the life of the individual.

Loyalty to the nation must be single-hearted and

not compromised by a loyalty to any other country. A person desiring citizenship in the United States, for instance, must renounce his allegiance to another nation and to any foreign sovereign. Such single-heartedness, however, does not prevent an interest in international order and in the well-being of other nations. Just as familial love and devotion do not preclude concern for those outside the family, loyalty to one's nation is compatible with an interest in alleviating the suffering of those in other parts of the world and in building a world of stability and progress.

History reminds us of many occasions on which American patriots made sacrifices both of their treasure and of their very lives in order to assist others throughout the world. One of the recent examples of this willingness to sacrifice for the freedom of others occurred in the years after World War II, when the United States not only sent relief aid to those whose lives had been ravaged by the war but also enabled the nations of both Europe and Asia—including defeated enemies—to rebuild their economies and to restore democracy and freedom where once tyranny had reigned. The meaning of patriotic loyalty translated into powerful forces for good in the world was expressed by George Santayana: "A man's feet must be planted in this country, but his eyes should survey the world."

Loyalty to the nation does not always mean loyalty to any given government. Patriotic loyalty may take the form of a conscientious stand against a regime that uses its coercive power to enforce its authority to oppress its own people. In this century, we have seen many heroic men and women who refused to surrender their consciences to tyrants and defied pernicious totalitarian governments. They answered the call to a higher loyalty to their nations when they sacrificed their lives rather than declare their allegiance to totalitarian rulers. (For a more detailed discussion of loyalty to the nation and to the government, see Cecil, *Three Sources of National Strength,* The University of Texas at Dallas, 1986, pp. 110–121.)

The fact that loyalty is a centralizing motive in an individual's personal life does not mean that it affects the development of the individual's conscience or of his moral will or that it excuses him from individual responsibility. An appeal to loyalty succeeds as a tool of oppression by tyrants only when an individual gives up his right to independent judgment. When a country is brutalized by a tyrant who demands loyalty from his oppressed subjects, the individual seeking freedom is guided by the vision of those who aspire to be free from tyranny. Only through such a vision can an individual attain spiritual fulfillment, a sense of solidarity with his fellowman, and inner peace.

Loyalty is an essential element in a democratic society. Anarchy without loyalty to any cause leads to apathy and a purposeless life, and destroys the social order that makes choices among causes possible. A totalitarian government destroys the individual who seeks an opportunity for freedom of choice and control. Although there is always the risk that one's loyalty may conflict with the loyalties of others, only in a democracy does one have a free choice among the countless causes that exist in a free society.

Loyalty to the nation, to the community where we live, to our family and friends is an integral part of our democratic institutions and the foundation of civil society. It provides the basis for the confidence that should subsist between those who are connected by the bonds of nationality, of a common community, of family, and of friendship—the dearest relationships in life. A steadfast loyalty cultivated in our social order enlightens our world by preserving the dignity of the individual, by giving him a sense of self-worth and a serenity of soul, combined with a recognition that his duties are a corollary to his rights. It is the solace of human existence.